The 10 Commitments
Parenting with Purpose

Chick Moorman and Thomas Haller, MDiv, MSW, DST

THE 10 COMMITMENTS
Parenting with Purpose

© 2005 by Chick Moorman, Thomas Haller, and Personal Power Press

Library of Congress Catalogue Card Number: 2004098929

ISBN 0-9616046-7-0

Printed in United States of America

Personal Power Press
P.O. Box 547
Merrill, MI 48637

Cover Design
Foster & Foster, Inc.—www.fostercovers.com

NEWSLETTERS

Chick Moorman and Thomas Haller publish FREE email newsletters for parents, educators, and couples. To subscribe to any one or to all three, email them at ipp57@aol.com. For back issues or further information and articles on parenting, teaching, and coupling, visit www.chickmoorman.com or www.thomashaller.com.

PARENT TALK FOCUS CARDS, by Chick Moorman ($10.00)

THE PARENT TALK SYSTEM: The Language of Response-Able Parenting, Facilitator's Manual, by Chick Moorman, Sarah Knapp, and Judith Minton ($300.00)

REDUCING FAMILY CONFLICT through Effective Parent Talk, videotape featuring Chick Moorman ($30.00)

"Moorman and Haller have given us a great gift in *The 10 Commitments*, an uplifting tribute to raising children."

Jim Fay
Author of *Parenting with Love and Logic*
Love and Logic® Institute, Inc.
Golden, CO

"In *The 10 Commitments*, Moorman and Haller have led us beyond parenting with consequences and discipline and into parenting that nourishes a child's spirit."

Elisa Medhus
Author of *Hearing Is Believing*

"*The 10 Commitments* is an inspirational blend of love, guidance, and instruction for the whole family. It will help you connect to your children soul to soul."

Jack Canfield
Co-author of Chicken Soup for the Soul® Series
Santa Barbara, CA

"What a heart-felt and developmentally sound parenting guide you have written. It is essential that we commit daily to the sacred and challenging role of parenting our children. You have outlined what I believe to be the key elements of guiding our children to become the very best they can be and I congratulate you sincerely for your beautiful work."

Maggie Dent
Author of *Saving Our Children from Our Chaotic World*
Dunsborough, West Australia

"Absolutely wonderful . . . these 10 Commitments are powerful and transforming. The impact that this book will have on families and the parent's role will be immeasurable."

Stephen L. Braveman, M.A., L.M.F.T., D.S.T.
Licensed Marriage & Family Therapist
AASECT Certified Diplomate of Sex Therapy
Monterey, CA

"I wish every new parent would read this book. It would help the parents and the children."

Judith Minton
Family Life Educator
Founder, Voice Works Seminars
Canton, MI

"*The 10 Commitments* is a sacred book. It contains powerful wisdom. It is truly inspirational."

Rev. Neltje Brawer
Kalamazoo, MI

"Transformational in nature. Use the 10 Commitments to transform your parenting style, your family relationships, and your attitude towards the important and sacred role of parenting."

Ivonne Delaflor
Founder of Mastery Life non-profit organization
Author of *The Positive Child through the Language of Love*
http://www.masterylife.com/
Cancun, Mexico

"Pay attention parents, grandparents, teachers—anyone who has anything to do with children anywhere—if you believe our future rests on our ability to raise caring, confident, self-responsible, empowered children and adults, Chick Moorman and Thomas Haller are the men who can show us all how."

Sandie Sedgbeer
Managing Editor
Children of the New Earth Magazine
www.childrenofthenewearth.com

"The 10 Commitments is a motivating book to help parents become the kind of parents they dreamed they would be. When parents ask me how they can help their daughters become confident, healthy and happy girls I will recommend reading this book."

Kimber Bishop-Yanke
President, Girls Empowered
(Birmingham) Detroit, MI

"This book will give you the tools you need to create a loving, emotionally healthy, connected family."

Lynn Gabriel
Early Childhood Outreach Liaison
Wausau School District
Wausau, WI

"If parents would take this book to heart and put these commitments into practice, their children will gain a stronger sense of self and be more equipped to handle life's challenges. I hope every parent reads it."

Tracey Thibodeau Serebin
Family Dynamics Consultant
A Child's Voice
Paramus, NJ

Contents

Introduction

Having a child changes your life like nothing that preceded it. You move instantly from being footloose to being child bound. Where once you stayed out and danced all night, your presence is now required for late night feedings or bedtime routines. Your budget, which was tilted heavily in favor of recreation, fun, and adventure, now includes line items for diapers and supplements, or, if your children are older, clothes, a lot more food in the refrigerator, and a college fund. What was once a simple trip to the mall now involves car seats and diaper bags or a carload of your child's adolescent friends.

The process of raising a child usually takes from 18 to 24 years. It involves making thousands of decisions and spending as many dollars. It demands a heavy investment of time, effort, and energy. It calls you to set aside your personal agenda and create a family agenda that meets the needs of all.

A major premise of *The 10 Commitments* is that parenting needs to be undertaken purposefully and with intentionality. It requires forethought, vision, and a sense of mission. It entails developing goals, clarifying values, and creating a parenting plan of action. It includes the belief that parenting is too important to leave to chance.

Not many prospective parents enroll in parenting classes and study parenting the way they would if they were going to tile the kitchen floor, remodel the basement, or install a new computer system in their home. Many, if not most, people parent unconsciously, without knowing why they behave in certain ways. Without any preconceived plan or intention, they parent by accident or happenstance.

9

Parenting with purpose involves making a commitment to yourself and to your children. This commitment is a pledge to be the best parent you can be for your child when he or she is an infant, toddler, adolescent, teenager, young adult, and mature adult; to provide nurture and structure when appropriate; to grow in parenting skill and knowledge; and to implement your parenting skills with love, firmness, and consistency.

Each chapter of the book includes a definition and overview of one of the commitments, followed by stories of real parents putting the commitment into practice in their lives. All of the names are fictitious, although the events and examples are real, drawn from incidents we have observed or been told about in our parenting seminars or professional practice. Following the real life stories, you will find a personal challenge. This is your opportunity to see where you stand on the commitment in question. Use this section of the chapter to check your beliefs about parenting and decide whether your behavior matches those beliefs.

This book is a celebration of parenting. Its intent is to encourage you to commit or recommit to your family and to the important role you play in the lives of your children. It offers ideas and techniques that will empower you as a parent. It is not an attempt to elicit guilt for parenting you have done in the past. Its goal is to encourage you to identify areas in your parenting life that you wish to celebrate and those you wish to change.

There is no one best place to begin implementing the ten commitments. There is no prescribed order to follow. You can start with the first commitment or with number ten. You can work on implementing one commitment exclusively or pick pieces of several commitments to put into practice in your family simultaneously.

As you read, look for sections that resonate for you. Find places that call you to take a closer look at your parenting philosophy and style. You will know where you need to begin. You will know what parts of your parenting need to be challenged and perhaps changed.

However you choose to parent after reading this book, do it with intentionality. Take active control of your parenting responsibilities. Make parenting with purpose your first commitment.

The 10 Commitments

The First Commitment

I commit to remembering that experience can be messy.

I accept that sand, mud, food, paint, cooking, eating, relationships, emotions, and social interactions can be messy. I allow my children to learn from making messes and the cleanup that follows. I recognize that experience can be messy.

The Second Commitment

I commit to creating a culture of accountability in my family.

I hold my children accountable for their actions and choices with gentleness and love. I implement consequences consistently and allow my children to experience the related, respectful, reality-based consequences that flow naturally from their actions. I create a culture of accountability.

The Third Commitment

I commit to suspending judgment.

I create an atmosphere in which mistakes are seen as learning experiences and valued for the lessons they bring. I perceive my children's choices as either appropriate or as opportunities for learning and development. I do not make my children wrong for

their choices, even as I hold them accountable for their actions. I suspend judgment.

The Fourth Commitment

I commit to managing my mind first.

I realize that how I approach a situation affects the outcome and that I alone control my approach. I attend to and manage my frame of mind before I approach my children. I move UP in my consciousness before I move IN with action. I manage my mind first.

The Fifth Commitment

I commit to focusing on the search for solutions.

I realize that fixing the problem is more important than fixing blame. I pledge to invest my time and effort in seeking solutions rather than in blame and punishment. I search for solutions.

The Sixth Commitment

I commit to speaking self-responsible language.

My language patterns reflect my belief in autonomy, personal responsibility, and ownership of one's actions and feelings. I learn and use language that helps my children see themselves as cause. I speak self-responsible language.

The Seventh Commitment

I commit to helping my children develop their inner authority.

I recognize that an inner authority is the only authority my children will take with them everywhere they go. To that end, I strive to make myself dispensable and to assist them in becoming increasingly in charge of themselves and their own lives. I help my children develop their inner authority.

The Eighth Commitment

I commit to modeling the message.

I recognize that attitudes are more easily caught than taught. I know that children pay more attention to what I do than to what I say. I walk my talk. I become the message I want to deliver to my children. I model the message.

The Ninth Commitment

I commit to seeing my child as teacher.

I recognize that my children are in my life as much so I can learn from them as they are so they can learn from me. I am open to the lessons my children offer me and honor them for helping me learn and grow. I see my child as teacher.

The Tenth Commitment

I commit to creating a sense of oneness in my family.

I am present for my children, helping them develop roots and feelings of belonging. I treat my children with love and caring. I create a sense of oneness in my family.

The First Commitment

I commit to remembering that experience can be messy.

I accept that sand, mud, food, paint, cooking, eating, relationships, emotions, and social interactions can be messy. I allow my children to learn from making messes and the cleanup that follows. I recognize that experience can be messy.

When a child is born, blood, placenta, amniotic fluid, mucus, sweat, and assorted other substances accompany the birth. It isn't long before the newborn fills his diaper with urine and feces. Drooling and spitting up follow. Everyone knows that babies make messes.

As children grow, evolve, and learn, messes continue. Toddlers get food all over their faces, the high chair, and the floor. Five year olds spill bath water on the bathroom floor. Eight year olds track in mud and sand. Twelve year olds wash white clothes with a red shirt and turn their socks and underwear pink. Fifteen year olds challenge authority and are given school detentions. Adult children make messes of their marriages or finances. Indeed, experience at any age can be, and often is, messy.

While experience can be messy, it can also lead to learning. Shoes that get soaked and pants that get muddy while collecting polliwogs from a nearby swamp are part of an experience that leads to increased understanding of life cycles as children watch polliwogs turn into frogs. Sand that gets tracked into the house results in your child learning how water and sand can be mixed to

create a myriad of structures which stimulate imaginative, creative play. Messy emotional outbursts from your teenager lead to learning which communication styles work and which ones don't.

Certainly, cleanup is necessary. The learning that occurs when your toddler removes all the pots and pans from the lower shelf to see how much noise they make can be supplemented by learning how to put them back. The mess that your son makes in his first attempt to bake chocolate chip cookies goes hand in hand with his learning how to clean up after himself when he is finished. The relationship mess your daughter's behavior creates with her grandfather leads to learning how to make appropriate amends when you have done something that offends or hurts another.

Depriving children of the right to make messes decreases their range of experience and limits their learning opportunities. Parents who allow children to make messes and hold them accountable for cleaning up extend opportunities that exceed those given to children who are required to be consistently neat, clean, and quiet.

Mess making also affords another important opportunity to parents— the chance to connect. Bonding occurs when you engage in water balloon fighting, finger painting, or drawing chalk pictures on the sidewalk with your children.

Connect with your children on their level. Get down on the floor and get messy together. Splash in rain puddles, cut and paste, take a radio apart with your daughter and see if the two of you can put it back together again. Initiate a watermelon seed–spitting contest in your backyard to see who can spit a seed the farthest. Paint, cook, hammer, and nail WITH your children. The mess is impermanent. It can be cleaned up and removed. The experience will stay with them forever.

Life Examples

Angelica became fascinated with her own feces when she was

36 months old. Because it came from her and was near her (usually in her diaper), she frequently put her hands in it. One time she smeared some in her hair.

Although her parents had many opportunities to respond to feces-related incidents, Angelica saved her finest feces moments for the childcare worker. One day, in the middle of a sweltering hot summer, Angelica pooped her pants. As the childcare worker attended to one of the other children under her care, Angelica decorated the screen door in the main entrance of the woman's home with her favorite decorating substance. She distributed her excrement into, over, and through the tiny holes of the screen as far as she could reach. The sight and the smell were indeed messy—so messy, in fact, that a hose, soap, water, and brushes could not totally dislodge it from the screen, which had to be replaced.

That night Angelica's parents counted their blessings that the screen-door feces experience did not happen in their home. Later that same night, Angelica became ill and threw up in her bed, proving that if you have children and you miss one mess, not to worry. Another is never far behind.

*****

Frank owned a home in the suburbs. He took great pride in how his house looked and was constantly touching up the paint job, washing windows, and tinkering about making small improvements. But as much as he loved his house, Frank's real pride and joy was his lawn. He had seeded it himself and he fertilized, watered, cut, and mulched it even before it needed it. His love for his lawn showed.

Lionel lived in the house next to Frank. His lawn was covered in divots where his children practiced hitting plastic golf balls with

their father's clubs. There were dead patches of grass along the bushes where the family dog often chose to pee. A huge worn area marked the spot where Lionel's son stood while bouncing a rubber ball against the front porch to practice his fielding skills.

One day, when both men were in their yards, Frank, standing by a freshly raked pile of leaves, asked Lionel, "How come you don't take better care of your lawn?"

Lionel paused for a moment and then replied, "Because I'm more interested in growing children than I am in growing grass."

*****

Corrine is a single parent with a ten-year-old autistic son. Every Saturday afternoon she takes him to the corner convenience store where they each purchase a Coke and a pretzel.

The Saturday afternoon ritual is usually a long, drawn-out process. Mark likes to pour his own drink, which is not easy for him to do. He often knocks over the cup, drops ice on the floor, and spills Coke on the counter. Occasionally, he drops his entire drink on the floor and has to start over.

Corrine could easily eliminate the confusion and the pending mess by doing it all herself, but she knows that Mark enjoys the opportunity to be independent. She views the Coke and pretzel adventure as a great experience for him. So now, whenever they head to the corner store for a Coke, Corrine tucks a roll of paper towels under her arm. She goes prepared because she knows the experience of letting Mark pour his own drink is messy.

*****

Martha's daughter, Andrea, came home from preschool with a note that stated: "This month the children have been learning about the colors of the rainbow. So far, we have learned the colors red, yellow,

and blue. This week we will be learning about the color purple. To help your child, please point out purple objects around your home. For Friday's Show and Tell, we would like your child to bring in something purple to share. Thank you."

Later that day, Martha sat down with Andrea to help her learn about colors. Andrea sat at the kitchen table in front of a big sheet of white paper and watched her mother pour a glob of red paint on one corner of the paper and a glob of blue on the other. Martha put several paintbrushes of various sizes in front of Andrea and suggested, "Let's paint."

Without hesitation, Andrea grabbed a paintbrush in each hand and began to swirl the brushes through the paint. Within minutes, the once white paper was covered in red and blue and, yes, purple.

Martha said, "Look! A new color. You made a new color." Amazed, Andrea dropped both paintbrushes and stared at her work. "You made the color purple," Martha told her daughter. "You mixed the red and the blue and made purple."

Andrea reached out and began to rub her hands through the purple paint. She asked for more red and blue paint and proceeded to make more purple. In her excitement, she got purple paint on the table, on her clothes, in her hair, on the floor, and on the dog as he walked by. Throughout it all, Martha sat calmly at the table and talked with Andrea about the color purple.

When Andrea was finished, her mom took her straight upstairs to the bathtub. In the tub, Andrea watched the water turn purple. After the bath, Andrea helped clean the kitchen table and the floor. As she did, the rag she used turned purple.

The next day, the children in Andrea's class shared purple objects during Show and Tell. The items brought from home included a plastic spoon, earmuffs, a coffee cup, a crayon, a mitten, socks, a pencil, assorted toys, a hat—and a picture created by a child who had discovered how to make her own purple.

*****

Brandon celebrated his seventh birthday by inviting six friends to stay overnight. Each showed up with a sleeping bag, pajamas, and a gift. Five of the gifts were beautifully wrapped, with crisp, even folds, an economical use of tape, and an attractive bow that was color coordinated with the wrapping paper.

The sixth gift was not totally covered with paper. The folds were ragged and an excessive amount of tape held it together. The bow was loose and looked as if it was about to fall off. As the child who brought the sixth gift handed it to Brandon, he smiled from ear to ear and proudly announced, "I wrapped it myself."

*****

Jim recently came home from work to find his two boys—Michael, age five, and Nate, age seven—standing at the back door to greet him. They were wearing yellow hardhats and tool belts. "Dad, duck down," they said. "We rewired the house. Come and see." Jim crouched down and crawled into the living room. In the corner chair sat his wife, calmly reading a magazine. Strung across the room from corner to corner and back again was red yarn. It was taped to the walls, chairs, couch, lamps, and windows in a spider-web pattern about three feet off the ground. It covered the entire living room.

Jim's wife looked up and said, "They've been working on this wiring project for a couple of hours."

"Yah," Michael said. "We're construction workers." Satisfied that their dad was enlightened as to the purpose of their efforts, the construction workers ran off to continue their "wiring" job.

Jim sat down next to his wife, smiled, and said, "What a mess!"

"Yes," she replied, "isn't it great?"

The house stayed wired for about a week as Michael and

Nate played out a different scenario each evening. At the end of the week, Jim helped the boys clean up the "construction site" as the crew prepared to move to a new location as well as a new learning adventure.

*****

While Josh and Trina wrapped holiday gifts, their three-year-old daughter, Amber, stood nearby with a pair of children's scissors. From an entire spool of ribbon, she began to cut half-inch pieces and let them fall to the floor.

Josh and Trina observed their daughter as they wrapped. They figured she would soon lose interest and move on to something else. Amber did not lose interest. She continued to cut. And cut. And cut. Perhaps she was imitating her parents. Maybe she just enjoyed cutting. Or she could have been fascinated with scissors. Whatever her motivation, she continued to cut until the entire spool lay at her feet in a heap of tiny pieces.

As her parents cleaned up their own scraps and put away their supplies, Amber did the same.

*****

Sixteen-year-old Clarissa Wilcox received a direct-mail-order offer to buy ten CDs for only $1.99. All she had to do was agree to buy six more at the regular price during the next year. Clarissa could hardly believe her good fortune and jumped at the offer. She asked her dad if he would write her a check if she gave him the cash.

Mr. Wilcox explained to Clarissa the dangers involved in agreeing to this deal. He knew from reading the offer that the CD company would send out a monthly announcement listing the featured selection as well as alternate selections and that if Clarissa didn't want any of those CDs she had to return a card within a limited time period.

He knew how easy it is to forget to send back the card and he carefully explained the way the system works to his daughter.

Clarissa chose to move ahead with the deal. The offer of ten CDs for $1.99 was simply too inviting to pass up. Besides, what could be so difficult about returning a selection card? she asked herself. Mr. Wilcox wrote the check and the deal was struck.

It took Clarissa about six months to create a minor money mess. By that time, she had received four CDs she didn't really want and had accumulated a debt of $47.50. To get out of the mess, she had to increase her babysitting commitment, wash her dad's car every other week for two months, and clean out her grandfather's garage.

Mr. Wilcox enjoyed the entire process. "Better to create a small mess now and learn from it," he told his wife, "than to learn a bigger lesson later when she gets her first credit card."

*****

Bonnie and Clara are next-door neighbors. They have two things in common that help them remain close friends. Each has a four-year-old daughter, and both love rummaging through garage sales looking for bargains.

On a recent garage sale excursion, Bonnie spied a paint easel that was in excellent condition and sported a four-dollar price tag. The easel, perfect for a budding preschool artist, was a bargain to be sure. Since Bonnie already had a paint area in her basement that included two easels, she signaled for Clara to come over and check it out.

"What is this?" Clara asked.

"It's an easel for painting," Bonnie told her. "It's perfect. It has places to hold six different paint jars and several brushes. And it's a real steal at four dollars."

"Why would I want this?" Clara wondered aloud.

"So Alisha can paint," Bonnie pointed out.

"Sounds kind of messy to me," Clara countered.

"Yes, it is," Bonnie agreed. "But the paint washes off and it's a great experience for kids. It would be perfect for a rainy-day activity."

"Paint drips and spills and gets tracked through the house," Clara told her friend. "Alisha makes enough messes without me asking for them by getting her something like this. Besides, she has plenty of videos she can watch when it rains. I'll pass."

Shortly after their conversation, Bonnie's van pulled away, leaving the easel behind. Later that day, it was purchased by a father who also bought two used shirts to serve as painting smocks—one for his daughter and the second for himself.

Experience Is Messy Challenge

Use this section to determine your tolerance level for mess. The areas below will help you assess where you are on commitment one. Determine your comfort level for mess and challenge yourself to stretch your present limits.

Cooking

Are you willing to let your children make a mess in the kitchen and learn how to clean it up? Do your children have the opportunity to burn a pizza, lick batter from mixers, crack their own eggs, spill flour, or design their own holiday cookies with sprinkles, M&Ms, raisins, and frosting?

Holidays

Do your children experience the squishy feel of the inside of a pumpkin as they dig out the seeds for Halloween? Do you arrange for them to string popcorn or cranberries to add to the Christmas tree? At Easter time, does your kitchen reflect the busyness of

children dipping eggs into colored cups of liquid to create age-appropriate designs?

Self-Involvement

Are you willing to build mud pies and get dirty along with your children? Have you jumped in a rain puddle next to your child lately? Have you rolled down a hill and gotten grass stains on your pants? Will you take off your shirt and let your son paint a tattoo on your chest? Do you take your kids to the water park and go down the water slides with them? Just how messy are you willing to get?

Letting a Mess Happen

Can you stand back and let your child pour a glass of milk for herself and watch what happens? Or do you jump in and do it for her so you don't have to deal with the mess? Will you let your young son put mustard on his own hotdog? Will you let your daughter experience putting grease on her bike chain without your help? To what degree will you allow a mess to happen?

Playfulness

Will you spray shaving cream on the kitchen table and enjoy watching what your child creates and learns? Are you willing to let your children cover the driveway in sidewalk chalk? Would you fill balloons half with water and half with shaving cream and surprise your kids as they get off the school bus? Will you run in the rain and slide in the grass? Will you rake leaves into a neat pile so you and your children can mess them up? Are you willing to have a "no manners" night at the dinner table once a month?

Creativity

Will you set your kids up with a bottle of glue, glitter, and tissue paper? Will you fill the kitchen sink with soapy water, add drops of food coloring, and let your daughter play in it? Will you keep the refrigerator box in the basement for the kids to cut, color, tape, and use for imaginative play? Will you allow your three year old to experiment with a roll of masking tape? Can you tolerate your teenage daughter coloring her own hair?

Independence

Will you allow your teenage son to choose the color of paint he wants in his room and encourage him to paint it himself? Will you let your daughter spend her weekly allowance any way she chooses and learn from mistakes she makes? Can you watch your four year old squeeze her own toothpaste onto her toothbrush without rushing to help?

Materials

Will you create a construction kit or a materials area for your children? Will it include tape, glue, staples, scissors, hammer, screwdriver, stickers, pens, paper, and sandpaper? Will you provide a place in your home where your children can use the construction kit regularly with appropriate supervision?

Pets

Can you stand the smell of cat litter? Does the thought of a dog digging and messing in your yard preclude your children having the opportunity to learn about love and care for an animal? Are you willing to put up with a hamster or a gerbil? What about a snake? Do thoughts of a foggy goldfish bowl keep you from helping your children learn about pet responsibilities?

Modeling

Do you make a mess in the garage when you build a birdhouse and follow through with cleanup? Do you get wet, dirty, and sweaty in front of your children when you wash the car, garden, mow the grass, and paint the garage? Do you show them how to clean your tools and pick up the leftover materials by doing it yourself?

Conclusion

Mess happens. If you have children, more mess happens. Get used to it. It's just the way it is. Your choice lies in how you view it. You can view a mess as awful, terrible, and disgusting. Or you can choose to see it as wonderful, exciting, and helpful.

How you choose to see a mess is important because it's your perception of it that determines your behavior. If you see messes as awful, you will likely do everything you can to prevent them, get angry if your children make them, work to keep things neat and tidy, and create stress for yourself when messes appear. You won't purchase that paint easel for your child, dump a load of sand in your backyard, or buy your kid a dog. You'll do all the cooking, laundry, and gift-wrapping. You'll discourage water balloon fights, playing in the rain, and eating in the car. You'll choose activities that are quiet, self-contained, and require no cleanup.

If you see a mess as helpful, you'll buy chalk, paint, and paste for your children. You'll construct a work area appropriate for mess making. You'll encourage cutting, gluing, stapling, and sawing. You'll organize trips to the swamp to collect bugs. You'll allow your children to fix you breakfast. You'll teach your children the importance of cleanup and hold them accountable for cleaning up their own messes.

Experience is indeed messy. As a parent, you get to choose the degree of mess you're willing to tolerate. Remember that at the same time you are choosing the range and depth of life experience in which your child will engage.

The Second Commitment

I commit to creating a culture of accountability in my family.

I hold my children accountable for their actions and choices with gentleness and love. I implement consequences consistently and allow my children to experience the related, respectful, reality-based consequences that flow naturally from their actions. I create a culture of accountability.

Creating a culture of accountability in your family involves developing a desire and a willingness to hold your children accountable for their actions by implementing reasonable, respectful consequences. It is a way of approaching discipline that allows children to experience both the negative and positive consequences of their choices and behaviors. Implemented consistently, with gentleness and love, consequences can become the cornerstone of your discipline structure and your children's path to developing responsibility.

Holding children accountable for their actions is one on the most loving things you can do as a parent. It is a way of telling your children, *I care about you.* It communicates, *I care about you so much I am willing to set limits and design consequences that evolve from the choices you make concerning those limits. In addition, I care enough to follow through with the consequences that your behaviors call for.*

Some parents think of a consequence as a form of punishment. They search for a consequence that will be strongly felt, thinking

that if it hurts in some way, the child will be sure to retain the lesson. We disagree.

What these parents don't understand is that it isn't the severity of a consequence that holds the impact. Consequences do not have to be severe. They only have to be certain. The certainty that specific, logical consequences follow actions allows children to trust the structure. Over time, they come to experience the structure provided by consequences as secure and are then able to relax into the clearly defined boundaries. Your consistency in implementing consequences is the glue that holds a culture of accountability together.

A consequence is a by-product of an earlier choice. It can be either a positive or a negative outcome. If you choose to skip lunch, the consequence will most likely be that of hunger later in the day. If your daughter chooses to leave her clothes on the floor of her bedroom rather than put them in the clothes hamper, the consequence is that the clothes don't get washed. If your son chooses to hang his coat on the hook inside the door as provided, the consequence is that he knows where his coat is the next time he heads out into the cold.

Some consequences have an immediate impact. If you pee your pants, you get wet and feel uncomfortable now. The effects of other consequences take time to accumulate. For example, if you choose to eat foods high in hydrogenated oils, the effects of the clogging in your arteries may not become evident for many years. If your son chooses not to brush his teeth, the effects may not be noticed for several months.

Whether consequences have immediate or delayed effects, it's important for us to help our children make the connection between their current choices and the outcomes those choices produce. Helping our children see the cause-and-effect relationship that exists between choices they make in their daily lives and the consequences that are directly related to those choices becomes a vital part of our parenting role and of our commitment to them.

One way of effectively structuring consequences so that children experience the relationship between cause and effect is to connect responsibilities to opportunities. A child of seven is given the opportunity to play with matchbox cars. She continues to earn the opportunity to play with the cars if she chooses to play with them responsibly. If she chooses to throw them, she loses the opportunity to play with them. With opportunity comes responsibility. If the responsibility is taken seriously, the opportunity continues. If the responsibility vanishes, so does the opportunity.

In a culture of accountability, opportunities are abundant. So are the responsibilities that come with each one. When the responsibility is not accepted, then the opportunity is temporarily lost. If you don't turn off the video game at the previously set time, then you lose the opportunity to play video games for a few days. If you don't come home by the agreed upon curfew, then you lose the opportunity to go out with your friends next time. If you visit computer websites that are considered off-limits, then you lose access to the computer for a period of time. The consequence is connected to the choice. By structuring the consequences around choices, you help your children experience the cause-and-effect nature of their choices and the results that follow.

Parents sometimes establish generic consequences that are unrelated to the behavior. "If you hit your brother, you can't use your Nintendo." "If you don't pick up your toys, you can't use your Nintendo." "If you talk back to me, you can't use your Nintendo."

When creating a culture of accountability, you need to relate the consequence more directly to the behavioral choice made by the child. "If you don't put gas in the car, you don't get the car on Friday." "If you drink all the Coke this weekend, you go without Coke the rest of the week." "If you choose to leave your toys out, I will put them on my top shelf until Sunday."

If a consequence is unrelated to the behavior, it is interpreted by the child's mind as punishment. The child's focus is then likely to

be on the person applying the punishment rather than on his or her choice of behavior. He's not thinking about what he could learn from his choice or what he could do differently next time. He's focused instead on the parent and on what is being "done" to him.

Another important consideration when creating a culture of accountability in your family is to keep consequences reasonable. Remember, a consequence does not have to hurt to be effective. It is not reasonable for a child to be "grounded" from his bike for a month because he failed to put it away one time. It is not reasonable for a young child's toys to be taken away for a week when she does not share them with her sibling. It is not reasonable to lose the chance to watch a favorite video for a week because the dishes were not washed. It is not reasonable to be grounded for two weeks because of a missed curfew. It is not reasonable to lose computer instant messenger privileges for the rest of a marking period because of low grades.

All of these consequences can be used effectively if applied in a more reasonable manner. Losing the opportunity to ride a bike for three days is reasonable. It also gives the child another opportunity to practice responsibility three days later, while the lesson is still fresh in his mind. Being grounded for the next weekend night, losing toys for two days, and losing instant messenger privileges until all missing assignments are turned in are reasonable consequences.

One goal of establishing and enforcing a consequence is to help the person experiencing it learn how to make a different choice next time. If the consequence is severe or unexpected, then the learning opportunity is likely to be lost as the person involved is caught up in feelings of hurt and anger.

In addition to consequences needing to be both related to the behavior and reasonable, they need to be administered in a respectful manner. When you talk to your child about opportunities, responsibilities, and related consequences, do it with respect and understanding. Set your feelings of anger or disappointment aside.

If you implement consequences with a strong tone of anger, children will tune into your anger rather than into the message you're attempting to deliver. Speak calmly, firmly, and seriously to the behavior that you want your child to learn to manage.

When implementing consequences, listen as well as speak. Be empathetic as you explain how opportunities were lost. Refrain from using words that attack character or personality. Speak to the situation with a tone that reflects serious concern but not catastrophe.

For many parents, creating consequences that are reasonable, related, and respectful is not difficult. Their difficulty occurs when it becomes time to follow through. It is easier to cave in than to hold their children accountable by following through with consequences.

In the moment, it may appear easier to extend the cleanup time one hour than to listen to whining and watch pouting when you announce the room did not pass inspection. But the lesson children learn from not being held accountable is, If I learn to pout and whine well, I can delay and often eliminate consequences. They also learn over time not to trust what you say. Since you don't follow through with consequences, your words eventually lose their meaning.

Please allow your children to experience the legitimate consequences of their choices and actions. Please do not rescue. Do not save. Do not bail them out.

Respect your child's right to choose and support his or her choice by following through with consequences firmly and consistently. Consequences that are enforced consistently help your child appreciate the relationship between cause and effect. They help children of all ages see themselves as capable of making choices. They help your youngsters see that the choices they make produce results. They motivate them to make responsible decisions. Consequences help children learn, *My choices created this; therefore, if I make different choices, I could create something else.*

Life Examples

When Brandon Hasleback bought his son Timmy a two-wheel bicycle for his seventh birthday, it did not come without responsibility attached. His father explained the situation this way: "You have opportunities and responsibilities with this bicycle, son. You have the opportunity to ride it in the neighborhood as long as you don't cross Western Avenue. That's too busy a street for bicycle riding. You also have the opportunity to use your bike throughout the day until it gets dark. When it gets dark, your responsibility is to see that your bike is put in the garage. It's important not to leave your bike outside overnight, where it could easily be stolen. Plus, I don't want to back out of the garage some morning and smash into it. If you take care of your responsibilities, you will keep earning the opportunity to ride your bike. If your level of responsibility drops, so will your level of opportunity."

After asking two clarifying questions, Timmy said he understood.

Three days later, Mr. Hasleback pulled into the driveway after dark and found his son's bike in the middle of his path to the garage. He immediately put the bicycle in the garage. Actually, he did more than put it in the garage. He hung it from ceiling hooks, far out of his son's reach.

At dinner, Timmy was informed that he had lost the opportunity to ride his bike for two days because he hadn't taken care of the responsibilities that went with it. "After two days you'll have another opportunity to use your bike responsibly," his father explained. "If you choose to handle your responsibilities well, you will continue to have the opportunity to ride."

Timmy knew his father was serious. He also knew he would soon get another opportunity to ride his bike. And he knew his opportunity to continue to ride his new bicycle was under his own control.

*****

Veronica and Tim returned home from their night out to find the babysitter very upset. She told them that their oldest son, Mark, age seven, had spent the evening calling her names and running from room to room hiding. He refused to play with his brother and even tried to engage the younger sibling in the name-calling. She described several techniques she used in an attempt to correct the behavior, including time out, loss of television privileges, and no evening snack. Nothing worked.

After hearing about his son's behavior, Tim asked the babysitter, "Can you come back tomorrow for about two hours?"

Hesitantly, she agreed.

That evening, after the babysitter left, Tim and Veronica sat down with Mark. Veronica began by explaining, "You had the opportunity to play and watch a video while your father and I went out. We got a babysitter so you and your brother could be safe and have fun playing together. It's not okay for you to call the babysitter hurtful names, run and hide, and be rude while she's here. Your responsibility is to play with your brother, listen to what the babysitter says, be safe with your body, and have fun."

Tim continued, "Mark, tomorrow the babysitter will be coming back and we'll do this a different way. You have lost the opportunity to be at the house with the babysitter and to play and have fun with your brother while she's here. Tomorrow when the babysitter is in our home, you will be with me and your mother while we go grocery shopping."

Mark whined, "I don't like going grocery shopping. It's no fun."

Veronica answered, "You made the decision to join us in grocery shopping by your choice of behavior tonight. Sorry."

When the babysitter arrived the next day, Mark pleaded with his parents to be allowed to stay home. He promised he would behave better and not act the way he had the night before. Even though Mark whined and cried, Veronica and Tim stuck to the

plan. Mark accompanied them to the supermarket.

On the way home in the car Mark asked, "Can I have an opportunity to be with the babysitter and be responsible next time?"

"Yes," Tim and Veronica replied in unison.

Sitting in the car in the driveway, Tim, Veronica and Mark talked about the responsibilities involved in staying at home when the babysitter was there. Mark agreed to the responsibilities and even suggested a couple himself.

Once inside, Mark asked the babysitter to return the next week so that he could have an opportunity to be different when she was watching him and his brother. She agreed.

The following week, Tim and Veronica went out to dinner while the boys had a "movie night" with popcorn and pop. The babysitter reported that both boys chose to use the opportunity to act responsibly.

*****

Esteban watched his adolescent son, Raul, engage in a fight during a soccer game. The two boys involved exchanged cuss words and physical blows. Both were ejected from the game and given a two-game suspension according to league rules.

Later that night, Raul complained to his father about how unfair the suspension was. "It wasn't my fault," he said. "He started it. He kept hitting me when the ref wasn't looking. I was just defending myself. I shouldn't have to miss the next two games."

Esteban waited calmly for his son to finish and then said, "My son, it is never OK to hit others. Regardless of who started it, you stayed involved by cussing and returning the blows."

Raul interrupted, "It's just like you to take their side. You never see things my way."

Esteban continued, "I'm not interested in taking a side. I am interested in you learning from this situation."

"I suppose you're not going to let me play soccer the rest of the season," Raul chimed in.

"No," Esteban said. "You will lose the opportunity to play in the next two games and can spend that time supporting your team from the sideline. Tonight you and I are going to talk about how to make a complaint to a ref when you're being mistreated on the soccer field and how to get the coach involved in the process." They spent the next hour doing just that.

During the next two games, Raul sat on the bench and paced the sidelines as Esteban watched the game from the stands as usual. When Raul turned to see if his father was still there, Esteban just smiled and nodded his head in approval.

*****

"This is your last chance," Brenda Johnson told her teenage daughter, Taryn, as she handed her the keys to the car. "If you don't put gas in the car tonight, you won't be able to use it tomorrow."

Brenda hoped she sounded like she meant it. She didn't like threatening her daughter, but simple reminders didn't seem to work. She didn't understand why Taryn couldn't remember something as important as gas. And she didn't like having to be the only one who put gas in the car.

Later that night, Taryn returned home with a gas tank that registered near empty. The following morning, when Brenda realized that the car needed gas, she drove it to the corner station and used her last seven dollars to purchase fuel. How many last chances is this kid going to need? she thought to herself.

After dinner, Brenda gave her daughter another lecture before she allowed her to take the car to visit a friend. She spoke sternly and said, "You won't get the car for a week if you don't put gas in it this time. And I'm not kidding."

*****

Kevin has two boys, ages seven and eight. They both love to jump. They jump on their beds, on the living room sofa, off the fireplace hearth, from kitchen chair to kitchen chair, down the stairs, over the dog, and up and down in place. They stack chairs on top of each other to make a higher platform from which to jump. Nothing, it seems, is off limits when it comes to jumping.

Since Kevin sees his boys only every other weekend, he doesn't like to impose too many rules. So he lets them jump. He also lets them stay up late, eat whatever they want—mostly junk food—and watch hours of television.

When confronted by his ex-wife about the difficulty she was having getting the boys to do their homework, go to bed at a reasonable time on school nights, and be respectful, Kevin exclaimed, "I don't have any of those problems when they're at my house."

"Of course not," the boys' mother replied. "You don't hold them accountable for anything."

"Why should I?" was Kevin's retort as he turned and walked away.

What is missing in Kevin's home is a culture of accountability. The lessons his children learn there (We can do whatever we want. If something gets broken, Dad will replace it. Any kind of food is OK for our bodies.) will certainly carry over into other areas of their lives.

Kevin's boys will eventually learn about cause and effect, but the lessons will most likely be embedded in much more difficult life situations.

*****

The middle school Lionel attends has a hot lunch policy that ensures that no one will go without lunch. Students pay in advance and get a full hot lunch each day from several choices provided as long as they have money in their lunch account. When the money gets low, students are warned and expected to inform their parents of the situation. If a student runs out of money, he or she is given a peanut butter sandwich and lettuce at no charge. They are not given a hot lunch.

Lionel's mother knows when he is about to run out of money. It would be easy for her to ask "Do you need more lunch money yet?" or "Aren't you about out of lunch money?" She asks no such questions. Instead, she waits for her son to do the asking. She believes her seventh grader is old enough to ask for lunch money when he needs it. She knows that if she makes lunch money *her* responsibility, it will never become *his*.

One week Lionel ate peanut butter sandwiches three days in a row. He forgot to tell his parents he needed money and suffered the consequences. When he got tired of peanut butter, he spoke up and got more lunch money. Lionel learned a lot from eating peanut butter. He learned that if he forgets to handle his responsibility he can cope, even though he isn't thrilled with the consequence. He also learned that he can control whether or not he gets a hot lunch. All he has to do is remember to take care of his responsibility.

*****

Ten-year-old Tamika talked her parents into buying her three goldfish by promising to be the person who fed the fish daily and who changed their water every two weeks. When the water-changing responsibility was ignored, Tamika's mother called a family meeting. Using problem-solving strategies, they came up with a plan Tamika could use to help her remember her responsibilities.

37

When the fish tank cleaning was neglected again, another family meeting was held. This time Tamika's mother explained that fish need food and clean water to live healthy lives. Without it they would probably die. "If you choose to feed the fish regularly and clean the fish tank on schedule, you'll be showing me that you're old enough and responsible enough for fish ownership. If you don't handle your responsibilities, someone else will have to do it. I will not sit back and watch fish die. And I'm not interested in doing it myself. What that means is that I'll have to find another owner who will keep these fish fed and able to swim in clean water." Tamika promised again to take care of the fish responsibilities.

Three weeks later, Tamika came home from school to find the fish and fish bowl gone from her bedroom. "What happened to my fish?" she asked her mother.

"I gave them away," her mother responded in a tone that communicated compassion and empathy. "I could see their water was dirty and I was worried they might die. I just can't watch a living thing die from neglect."

Tamika cried in her bedroom for 30 minutes, intermittently begging her mom to reconsider. Her mom remained firm and the fish remained gone.

Culture of Accountability Challenge

Look through the items below. Decide if you are pleased with the amount of accountability you have created in your family regarding each of them. Challenge yourself to strengthen the culture of accountability in your home by increasing your efforts in several areas. Pat yourself on the back where you find issues you have firmly in place in your family.

Natural Consequences

Do you allow a natural consequence to occur or do you step in to rescue your children from experiencing the effects of their choices? Will you allow your daughter to forget her swimsuit on the day the gym class gets to use the pool? Will you allow your son's lunch box to sit on the counter as he steps out the door to catch the school bus? Can you stand aside and let the consequence do the teaching?

Reasonable

Are you reasonable in the application of consequences, or do you create consequences that are severe? Do you ground your teenager for a month or throw the Game Boy in the garbage when grades fall below expectations? Can you let go of seeing a consequence as something that has to hurt severely to be effective?

Related

Can you develop a consequence that is directly related to the choice? Or do you rely on one or two generic consequences that don't help children see the direct connection between their behavior and the results that follow?

Respectful

Do you use words and a tone of voice that reflect love and gentleness when you present a consequence to your child? Do you avoid words that send an underlying message that he or she is wrong or not good enough? Can you set your feelings of anger or disappointment aside and speak to the behavior that you want your child to learn to manage? Do your behavior, your words, and your tone reflect a belief that holding children accountable is one of the most loving things you can do as a parent?

Responsibilities

Are you able to connect opportunities to responsibilities when you implement consequences? When your children fail to follow through on a responsibility, do you help them experience a loss of opportunity? Do you talk to them about the important connection between opportunities and responsibilities?

Follow Through

Do you follow through and stick to the consequence you set, or do you let it slide "this time"? Do you rescue, save, and bail out your children, figuring that they'll do better next time because you were nice to them and cut them some slack? What degree of consistency do your children expect from you based on your past behavior in following through on an agreed-upon behavior or rule? Do you say what you'll do and then do what you said consistently?

Accountability

Do you hold your children accountable for the choices they make? Do you hold yourself accountable for the choices *you* make? Do you take responsibility for your actions? Have you developed a culture of accountability within your family?

Conclusion

Creating a culture of accountability in your family is a simple process. It involves giving your children choices and allowing them to experience the positive and negative consequences that flow from those choices. It requires that you follow through consistently and trust the process of designing and implementing consequences.

When you commit to creating a culture of accountability, you trust that your children can learn as much from the consequence as

they can from you. You believe that by regularly holding your children accountable they will learn to see themselves as the cause of the results they produce. You know that by helping them experience the direct relationship between cause and effect they will become more empowered and view themselves as both capable and responsible.

The Third Commitment

I commit to suspending judgment.

I create an atmosphere in which mistakes are seen as learning experiences and valued for the lessons they bring. I perceive my children's choices as either appropriate or as opportunities for learning and development. I do not make my children wrong for their choices even as I hold them accountable for their actions. I suspend judgment.

Children make mistakes. They make mistakes learning to walk. They make mistakes learning to talk. They make mistakes with their homework. They make mistakes with relationships. And they make mistakes in responsibility.

To commit to the principle of suspended judgment means to assign no positive or negative value to mistakes. It means refusing to see mistakes as good or bad. It means perceiving them instead as choices that offer opportunities for growth.

Parents who suspend judgment do not name a behavior a "mistake" or judge it until they see how the child chooses to use it. If your child gets a speeding ticket, is confronted with the consequences, and then uses that experience to slow her driving, was getting the ticket a good thing or a bad thing? If your child forgets to put his bike away and loses the opportunity to use it for a few days and learns to see himself as the cause, is forgetting to put the bike away good or bad?

The commitment to suspend judgment calls upon parents to wait and observe the "mistake." None of us knows the master

plan. We have no way of knowing how the mistake will be used. In addition, we don't always know what our child is attempting to learn. Our job is to support our children in learning about themselves and the world around them. To do that effectively, we must set aside preconceived ideas about their choices and suspend judgment. In that way, we allow our children to teach themselves through their behaviors and the resulting outcomes.

Allow the child's choice and the outcome of that choice to be the teacher. With helpful debriefing, growth will occur as the child moves through the "mistake" to learning. Our role is to create an atmosphere in which mistakes are not only permitted but are seen as exciting opportunities for learning to occur.

Creating this type of atmosphere does not mean we want you to ignore health and safety issues. Children are not allowed to play in the road so they can learn that cars hurt. Poisonous chemicals are not left out so children can learn of their dangers through personal experience. Plug covers are not removed so children can learn about electricity using a "hands on" style of learning.

Car seats and seatbelts are used without exception or debate. Staying up until 3:00 a.m. on a school night is not allowed. A sixteen year old driving four friends to school is not permitted. These choices are not safe or healthy. Do not set up your family environment so children can learn lessons from these mistakes. The price they pay is simply too high.

Search for a safe way to help your child learn important lessons that could have life-threatening consequences. A sixteen year old can drive one friend to school instead of four. Staying up until 3:00 a.m. can occur on special occasions such as prom night. Food coloring, salt, flour, and cereal can be mixed to create mysterious concoctions that are not poisonous. Health and safety concerns are not to be suspended. What needs to be suspended is judgment as children learn by making minor "mistakes" that do not compromise their health and safety.

Occasionally, children need to get what appears to be "off course" before they get back "on course." Refuse to see "off course" as good or bad. Don't even choose to see it as "off course." See the situation as on course for that child—on course for receiving the perfect feedback he needs to determine the next step on his individual path toward creating who he is becoming.

Another way to suspend judgment is to learn to separate the deed from the doer. Children are not their behavior. They are not their anger. They are not their report card. They are not their table manners. Their behavior is simply their behavior—what they are choosing to do in the present moment. It is not who or what they are as a human being.

In a recent workshop, Transforming Aggression in Children, a parent described her daughter with the words, "She's a tyrant. Whenever she wants my attention, she becomes a monster who terrorizes her little brother." By describing her daughter this way, this mother has equated her daughter with the behavior. She has connected the deed to the doer, and, in her head, the daughter *is* a monster.

This child is not a monster. She is a young child choosing aggressive behavior in a particular moment. She is a child demonstrating a lack of skill in knowing how to ask for what she wants or needs.

Holding children accountable for their actions without making them wrong is yet another way to suspend judgment. If your teen fails to put the agreed-upon gas in the car, don't make him wrong. Don't make him cheap. Don't make him forgetful, lazy, or bad. Just make him someone who doesn't get the car for a few days. If your twins color the kitchen wall with markers, don't make them wrong. Don't make them bad, dumb, or unthinking. Instead, make them twins who get a lesson in how to clean markers off walls.

Making children wrong for their behaviors creates resistance. To create an emotionally safe family space where your children

can look at their behaviors and learn from them, suspend judgment and avoid right/wrong thinking. By removing right and wrong from the equation, you help children focus on their behavior and the results those behaviors produce.

Beware of the judgment trap. Judging children as unorganized, uncoordinated, athletic, artistic, rude, motivated, or obnoxious places them in categories that leave little room for deviation. Your judgments will limit your vision and narrow your perspective, trapping your children in boxes that serve to confine and control.

Judgment makes permanent. Judging and labeling your child as lazy, disrespectful, or spoiled tends to be self-fulfilling. If you judge your child as lazy and use language and behavior that communicates that belief to her, you increase the chance that she will act in ways that match your belief. When you then notice those behaviors, your beliefs grow even stronger.

Instead of judging children, why not see them as unfinished? Regardless of their age, your children are still unfolding. Perceive them as "not yet done." They are busy learning, growing, and taking part in a journey that will transform them into the adults they will soon become. And they can do that best when you help them by suspending judgment.

Life Examples

Lionel's mother wanted him to take band in sixth grade. She had been a band member in school and found it to be a rewarding experience. She enjoyed the trips, the performing, and the camaraderie that developed. So Lionel began sixth grade equipped with a flute and an assurance that he would love band.

Lionel did not love band. In fact, he hated it. Getting him to practice was a chore. On occasion, he forgot to take his instrument to school. Many times he forgot to bring it home.

Lionel stuck it out in band for two years, mainly because he

45

knew it meant so much to his mother. In ninth grade, he asked to quit. Lionel's mom was distraught. "This is terrible," she told her friends. "If I let him quit, he'll never grow to appreciate music." In her mind, his desire to quit was wrong, a bad decision that would surely lead to a life without music.

Lionel quit band. After he graduated from high school, he got a job as a clerk in a music store. He developed a taste for alternative rock music. In fact, he liked it so much he taught himself to play the bass guitar and formed a rock band. Lionel managed that band for three years. In addition to music skills, he learned organizational, marketing, and interpersonal skills that he would use throughout his life. Today, music remains an integral part of Lionel's life.

*****

Ryan Hobbes took his daughter Madison shopping for back-to-school shoes two weeks before she entered first grade. Madison had in her head a certain style of shoe she wanted. Her father had in his head a certain price range he was willing to pay. Being a bright girl, it didn't take long for Madison to figure out there was a difference between what she wanted and what she was likely to get.

In an attempt to tip the scales toward her shoe preference, Madison chose a well-known behavior. In the middle of a shoe store in her hometown mall, she threw a temper tantrum. And it was a good one. She sprawled on the floor, kicked her feet, wiggled her arms, and rolled over a couple of times, crying and mumbling unintelligibly about shoes.

Madison's dad decided to take action, but before he did, he reminded himself that his daughter had a positive intention: to get the style of shoes she wanted. Nothing is wrong with that intention, he told himself. He had the same intention every time he bought shoes for himself. What he didn't appreciate was the behavior Madison chose in an attempt to fulfill her positive intention.

Bending down close enough for his daughter to hear, Mr. Hobbes said, "You sure look angry. I see you kicking and wiggling. I can hear your loud sobs. You must be really frustrated."

When he finished, Madison looked up and made eye contact. That was the signal her father was waiting for. "You have two choices," Ryan told his daughter at that point. "You can choose to keep kicking and crying and end our shopping trip. Or you can choose to stop crying and get up off the floor and we'll continue to shop. Those are your choices."

Before Madison could respond, her father added a key piece to his parenting effort. He used his verbal skills to separate the deed from the doer. "I love you," he told her, "and I don't enjoy shopping with people who choose to lie on the floor and kick and cry. It's not you I don't like, Madison. It's the behavior. I don't enjoy shopping with anyone who chooses this behavior. So you decide if you want to continue shopping or go home and try again in a few weeks. You choose."

Whether Madison kept on with her tantrum is irrelevant. It doesn't matter if she continued her tantrum and chose to go home or ended it and chose to shop. What is important is that she was empowered by having her choices clarified for her, and she was given the opportunity to see herself as more than her behavior.

*****

As Jim walked into the school office, he could hear his son screaming in the adjoining room, "No, I won't go! I won't let go of the desk! Leave me alone!"

The school secretary pointed to the door and mouthed the words, "Go in." Jim opened the door to find his ten-year-old son, Tony, sitting on the floor holding tightly to the corner of the principal's desk. The exasperated principal stammered, "He's suspended. Get him out of here and don't bring him back for two days!"

The principal handed Jim a suspension slip with a note from Mr. Howard, Tony's teacher, describing what Tony had done. According to the note, Mr. Howard had been called from the room, and when he returned he found Tony standing on a chair "clowning around." The note said that Tony refused to leave the room when he was ordered to go and that he argued that he was not clowning around. The report went on to say that Tony became disrespectful to the teacher and that was why he was being sent to the office.

The suspension slip also included a note from the principal. He cited Tony's disrespectful behavior in the office, including his loud, argumentative, and angry tone. The principal wrote that Tony refused to sit in the chair as told and that he kept yelling, "I didn't do anything wrong."

Jim calmly sat down on the floor next to his son and said, "My son, tell me what happened from your point of view. How did all this get started for you?"

With tears in his eyes and a cracking voice, Tony explained. "The girl I was sitting next to was having trouble seeing her paper because the sun was shining in her eyes. She tried to close the shade a little, but it got stuck. I stepped up on the chair to fix the shade just as Mr. Howard walked in. He yelled at me right away, saying I knew better than that, and he told me to go out in the hall. He never gave me a chance to explain that I was trying to help. Nobody did." Tony lowered his head and said, "Then I just got mad."

Jim helped his son to his feet and escorted him out the door. As he did, he looked at the principal and said, "I'll be back tomorrow to talk with you further about this incident."

If Mr. Howard had suspended judgment for a brief moment, he could have learned about Tony's intentions. He could even have assisted Tony by holding the chair as Tony released the shade. He could have seized the moment and involved the entire class in brainstorming other ways to solve the problem in a safe and helpful manner.

By suspending judgment, Mr. Howard could have created a different scenario and outcome. Instead, he gave Tony an opportunity to learn how to manage his anger and how to present his opinion effectively to those who are quick to pass judgment.

*****

At the midyear parent-teacher conference, Arlene was alarmed to learn that her second-grade son had not taken a single Accelerated Reader test. The teacher explained that Mark had many opportunities to take the test but he still had 0 points and that he needed 25 points to participate in the classroom reward of attending a movie at the end of the year. She was insistent that something be done as soon as possible and suggested that Mark stay in from recess twice a week and begin taking AR tests. She gave Arlene a list of books that were a part of the AR program and encouraged her to have Mark read from that list.

Arlene was somewhat puzzled, since she frequently observed Mark reading. As soon as she returned home, she talked with Mark about the AR book list. She discovered that he had read most of the books on the list. When she inquired as to why he hadn't taken any of the tests, he replied, "I read because I like to read, not because I want points or want to go to a movie."

"Other kids will get to go to the movie and you won't. You might have to stay at school and do other work," his mother told him.

"I know. I don't care" was Mark's response.

Arlene thought for a moment and then replied, "Let's see how that works for you." She set the matter aside and waited to see what lesson, if any, Mark's choice would present to him.

*****

Margaret walked in the door from work to find her daughter waiting in the living room. Elivia wasted no time in saying, "Mom, we need to talk."

There was a moment of silence as Margaret sat down. "What happened?" she asked.

"Well, I'm not sure, but I think I'm pregnant."

Margaret stood up immediately. "What? You think you're pregnant? You had sex with that boy, Marcos? You're fifteen. What were you thinking? I can't believe you would do this to yourself and to us. How long have you been having sex with him? Oh, I don't want to know! I just can't believe you could be so stupid, after all we've taught you." Margaret threw up her hands and walked out of the room.

Unsure of what to do next and with tears running down her face, Elivia walked out the back door.

Later that evening Margaret and her husband spent several hours frantically searching for their daughter. After calling all her friends and the police station, they received a phone call from Elivia's English teacher, who had returned home from a late movie with her husband to find Elivia sitting on her front porch. After talking with her teacher for close to an hour, Elivia finally decided to call home and see if her parents were ready to listen to her.

Margaret missed a chance to join her daughter in the initial stages of this learning opportunity. Later, she was able to stop fixing blame and start addressing the problem but, sadly, because of her judgmental attitude, her relationship with her daughter was never the same again. At the age of 25 and with a college degree behind her, Elivia still hesitates to share personal information with her mother. She fears being judged.

*****

Benny graduated from high school with a 1.98 Grade Point Average. He enrolled in a state university in the Midwest. After he had spent three semesters of half-hearted college effort, Benny and the university arrived at the same conclusion. He dropped out the same day he was asked to leave.

Benny's parents were more than disappointed. They were furious. They were sure Benny was ruining his life. "Nobody gets anywhere without a college education these days," his father scolded. "You won't be able to get a decent job," his mom assured him. They were convinced Benny was making bad decisions about his life that he would rue later on.

Benny moved out. He worked in a fast-food restaurant for six months. He sold clothes for a store in the mall. For one year, he worked as a car salesman for a local car dealership. After three years of low-paying odd jobs, he decided to go back to school.

Benny did not decide to return to school because of anything his parents said. He made that decision because he realized it wasn't fun to sell cars, clothes, or hamburgers. He wanted to do something with his life that gave him a greater sense of purpose.

Benny got back in college under probation. After one year, he was not only off probation, he was on the Dean's List. Two years after that, he graduated. Today he is a middle-school teacher making a difference in the lives of seventh- and eighth-graders.

*****

Eight-year-old Reed started out the door dressed for the snow that had fallen the previous night. He was ready for school and looked forward to recess later that day. As he passed his father with his book bag in hand, his dad inquired, "Do you have your shoes in there for when you get to school?" With a roll of his eyes, Reed snapped, "Yessss!"

Off to school Reed and his dad went, kicking snow at each other along the three-block walk. On the return walk home, his father received a call on his cell phone.

"Hey, Dad, I can't find my shoes. I thought they were in my book bag and now they're not there. Can you check at home and bring them back to me?"

As he walked on, Reed's father replied, "That's an interesting choice you've made. You can see where you left your shoes when you get home tonight."

"But, Dad! I can't go all day without my shoes."

"You'll think of something. I'll see you tonight, my son," his father said as he turned off the phone.

Very little discussion took place that night. Reed found his shoes on the floor by the back door—right where he had left them. His father said nothing. He was not the teacher of this lesson.

*****

Juan was eight years old when he received a silver aluminum scooter for his birthday. He loved it and spent hours scooting back and forth on the sidewalks near his home.

The first time Juan's father saw him using the scooter without wearing shoes, he took action. He didn't wait for Juan to experience the natural consequence of damaging his toes by scraping them on the sidewalk. His first priority as a parent was the health and safety of his children.

"Using a scooter barefooted is dangerous," he explained to his son. "It's important that you always wear shoes when you use your scooter. The shoes protect your feet and keep them free of scrapes, bruises, and serious injury." This concerned parent went on to explain, "You have the opportunity to ride your scooter all over the neighborhood. With that opportunity comes responsibility. If you choose to take the responsibility, you choose to continue the

opportunity. If you neglect the responsibility, you choose to give up the opportunity. Do you understand?" Juan assured his father that he did.

Two weeks later, Juan's father noticed his shoeless son on the scooter. Again, he did not allow the natural consequences to kick in. He did not permit his son to injure himself through his choice to ride barefooted. Instead, he implemented consequences.

"Please put your scooter in the basement," Juan's father told him. "In this family, responsibilities equal opportunities. When the handling of responsibilities lessens, so do the opportunities." This parent did not make his son wrong. He did not make him bad. He did not make him forgetful. He did not make him lazy. He did, however, make him someone who would be without a scooter for a few days.

The Suspended Judgment Challenge

How are you at suspending judgment? Are you ready to accept the third commitment as part of your parenting profile? As you look through the items below, check yourself and the environment you are creating around your children. Does the atmosphere reflect the third commitment? Make changes in your family structure as you learn and grow through your learning opportunities.

Judgment

Do you see behavior as good or bad, right or wrong? Is there such a thing as a "bad" choice, or was the choice perfect for learning what needed to be learned? Does your behavior match your answer? Do you expand your children's vision and broaden their perspective by eliminating words that judge?

Labeling

Do you label your children? Do you see them as spoiled, lazy, rude or obnoxious, or as outgoing, athletic, motivated, kind, polite? Positive or negative, a label is a label. Are you increasing the odds that your children will live up to the label you provide for them? Or are you letting them grow past the label while creating their own vision of themselves?

Allowing

Will you allow learning to happen, or do you have to be the one who teaches everything your child learns? Can you let the lesson be in the choice and the result it produces? Are you willing to wait for the outcome of a choice, even if it takes a couple of months or years? Can you say, "Let's see how that works for you," even when you suspect what the result will be from your prior experience? Can you wait to see how a child will use the "mistake" she made?

Mindset

Can you allow your mind to see mistakes as opportunities for growth and learning? Can you cultivate an attitude that helps you separate the deed from the doer as you implement consequences? Can you create the belief that "mistakes" are not good or bad, right or wrong? Can you approach a discipline session knowing that how the "mistake" is used is the most important ingredient?

Beliefs

Do you believe that children know what they need to learn and that they will make choices that help them learn it? Or do you believe that you need to personally teach your children each lesson? Do you believe that learning can happen when you are not present to instruct—that learning can occur through the natural course of an

event? Do you believe that your children are on a journey that will transform them into adults? Will you always be there to help them on that journey?

Modeling

Are you willing to make mistakes and to learn and grow from them? Do you let your children see your mistakes, or do you work at being perceived as flawless in their eyes? Do you admit when you make a mistake, or do you model for your children how to come up with good excuses? Do you publicly beat yourself up for the mistakes you make, or do you see them as valuable for the lessons they offer?

Conclusion

A primary component of the principle of suspended judgment is *Mistakes are permitted here.* That component can best be implemented in your family when you refuse to see mistakes as good or bad, when you apply consequences without making your children wrong for their actions, and when you steer clear of the judgment trap by refusing to label and categorize their behaviors.

What are your present thoughts about the third commitment? Are you judging it as wrong, impractical, or not right for your family? If so, you are caught in the judgment trap. Why not suspend judgment on suspending judgment, play with the concept, and see what happens? You might be surprised by the results.

The Fourth Commitment

I commit to managing my mind first.

I realize that how I approach a situation affects the outcome and that I alone control my approach. I attend to and manage my frame of mind before I approach my children. I move UP in my consciousness before I move IN with action. I manage my mind first.

Parents are managers. We manage time, temperature, calories, furniture, schedules, chores, money, routines, television programming, computer access, the interaction patterns of our children, and much more. While as parents we are called upon to make thousands of management decisions daily, most of us fail to make conscious and purposeful decisions in the one area that could have the greatest influence on our children. We neglect to manage our own minds.

A commitment to managing your mind involves purposefully creating your own best picture of yourself as a parent and then paying attention to whether or not your behavior and language are congruent with that picture. It also includes investing the time necessary to assess, and change if necessary, your present state of mind before engaging conflict, implementing consequences, or making important parenting decisions.

We create who we want to be as a parent first in thought and then in deed. By thinking about and choosing the principles under which you want to function ahead of time, you increase the likelihood that you will maintain your chosen posture and not be thrown off

later by the behavior of your child. Managing your mind by creating your best picture of yourself as a parent will help you respond to the behavior with actions that fit your desired picture of yourself.

Create a preferred image of yourself responding to your child as she is having a tantrum or telling you to shut up. Build a positive picture in your mind of the next step you would take when your child is whining or refusing to go to bed at the designated time. With the desired vision of yourself firmly in mind, observe your tone of voice, your body posture, your facial expressions, your intentions, and what you're modeling to your child. Creating and holding that vision will help you choose actions that are congruent with it. Once your personal vision of the parent you want to be is in place, you will be ready for action.

One important aspect of managing your own mind is learning to move UP in your consciousness before you move IN with your action. When your daughter runs over your prize tulips with the lawn mower, when your toddler spills milk at the dinner table, when your teenage son comes home late—action is called for. To ensure that the action you take flows from love as well as from logic, pause. Take three deep breaths and actively change your frame of mind before you respond.

To help you move UP before you move IN, we recommend six strategies:

1. Talk to yourself before you talk to your child.
2. Make a BE choice before you make a DO choice.
3. See it all as perfect.
4. Accept that what is . . . is.
5. Look for the gift.
6. Make no assumptions.

Talk to yourself before you talk to your child.

To honor your commitment to manage your mind first, talk to yourself before you talk to your child. By paying attention to your thoughts and purposefully shaping the conversation you have with yourself, you take charge of your attitude, your energy, and your relationship to the parenting moment that is before you.

Using encouraging self-talk is one way to effectively take charge and manage your own mind. Encouraging self-talk helps you to create the frame of mind you desire rather than leave that important function to chance. For example:

- I don't have to take this personally. My child's choices do not mean that I'm a good parent or a bad one. This isn't about me. It's about him and where he currently is on the learning curve.
- This behavior is age appropriate. Three year olds mark on the walls with crayons. Some ten year olds wet the bed. Teenagers activate power struggles. Even though I don't like this particular behavior, it's normal for my child's age.
- Helpful lessons spring from uncomfortable situations. This situation has the potential to create learning and healing.

Refuse to let whatever thoughts initially spring into your mind control you when a potentially stressful parenting situation presents itself. Notice your thoughts and change them if you choose. You can rise above any situation and bring calm and peace to it by using helpful self-talk. Activate this mind skill often to help you become the parent you truly want to be.

Make a BE choice before you make a DO choice.

As parents, we make DO choices regularly. Activities we sometimes decide to do with our children include playing catch, going to a movie,

going out for ice cream, cleaning the garage, giving a lecture, putting a child in time-out, roasting marshmallows, reading a bedtime story, playing a game of Monopoly, and settling an argument between siblings. Most parents are familiar with the concept of making DO choices.

Not as familiar to many parents is the concept of making a BE choice. A BE choice occurs when you purposefully choose how you are going to BE when you do whatever it is that you decide to do.

When reading a bedtime story, for instance, you could choose to BE silly, emphatic, serious, demonstrative, quick, humorous, childlike, or lively. How you choose to BE will dramatically alter the experience of the bedtime story. If you don't think so, be silly one night and serious the next. You will feel and see the difference and the impact each choice has on your child.

If the task is to discuss poor grades on a report card with your daughter, that is your DO choice. We suggest you decide how you want to BE before you activate your DO choice of engaging in the discussion. You could choose to be firm, confrontational, empathetic, sincere, friendly, loving, surprised, thorough, open-minded, inquisitive, or a variety of other options. By making a BE choice, you shape your experience of discussing the report card. Your behavior will flow from your choice of how to BE and adjust to fit that form. In essence, you have managed your mind to create a desired result.

See it all as perfect.

Another mind management technique you can use to move up in your consciousness is to choose to see your present circumstances as perfect.

If your child is disrespectful to her grandparent, why not see that situation as the perfect way for your daughter to communicate

to you that she needs to learn more about respect for the elderly? It is also the perfect time and the perfect opportunity for you to teach a lesson on respect.

When your child leaves his toys out, that is the perfect time for him to learn about what happens when he makes that choice. If your teen turns off the alarm and goes back to sleep, that becomes the perfect opportunity to allow her to experience the natural consequences of being late for school. If the dishes are stacked up in the kitchen, that's the perfect time to delay dinner until the kitchen is in order.

Choose to view these events as opportunities for you to practice moving UP before you move IN. They are the perfect situations you need to help you practice this skill. Welcome them.

Accept that what is . . . is.

Another "Move UP before you move IN" technique is to accept that what is . . . is. If you find yourself thinking that things should be other than they are—that the children should be different, that they should know better, or that you should have done something differently—you are emotionally resisting and fighting what is.

The *fact* is that your twins did decorate your kitchen wall with permanent markers. That's *what is*. No amount of anger, frustration, noise, or irritation will change that. The wall is the wall and it is covered with permanent marker.

Yes, work to make changes on the physical level. Teach the necessary lessons to encourage that different markers be used on a different surface next time. Involve your children in cleanup. Implement appropriate consequences if necessary. Dealing with the situation on the physical level is important and necessary—and that part of parenting can be handled more effectively when you emotionally accept your present-moment circumstances.

Look for the gift.

Another way to manage your mind and move UP before you move IN is to look for and find the gift that is present in each situation.

As you stay home with your sick child, your mind may send you messages of "poor me" and "this isn't fair." Your mind is taking the victim stance by generating limiting thoughts and concentrating on negativity.

Change your mind about your present circumstance by looking for the gift that it offers. It could be an opportunity to clean out a closet, wash the car, or catch up on thank you notes. Perhaps there is a gift waiting for you in a chance to snuggle with your daughter and watch a video. Maybe your gift arrives as a change in routine, a day off work, or time to play your guitar. The gift is there. It's up to you to train your mind to find it.

Make no assumptions.

Beware of the assumption trap. As parents, we think we know. We think we know why our child lied to us. We think we know what she is thinking. We think we know what he is about to do next. We think we know who began the fight in the next room. To move UP before you move IN, free your mind of assumptions.

If you remind your ten year old about his responsibilities with the garbage and he turns and walks away, you assume he didn't hear you or that he heard and doesn't care. With your assumption firmly in place, you use a tone and volume in your next communication that escalates the incident. Before you can find out your son was on his way to get his shoes so he could take the garbage out to the road, the situation sinks to a lower level, careening out of control in a downward spiral.

Allowing assumptions to control your mind leads to conflict and misunderstanding. To manage your mind effectively in important

parenting situations, it is necessary to refrain from making assumptions. Tell yourself: I may not know for sure what is going on here. I will keep an open mind. Understanding is my top priority. Keep your commitment to manage your mind first by entering crucial parenting moments free of assumptions.

Life Examples

Brandon Stewart was feeling put upon. He had driven his son, Tevi, to the doctor, sat in the office for an hour, gone in with his boy to see the doctor, and was now driving across town to deliver the prescription to the pharmacy. He knew he would have to wait while the prescription was filled, drive home with a coughing ten year old sitting next to him in the front seat, and then convince the youngster to take the medicine. He felt used up and worn down.

While waiting for the pharmacist to do her job, Brandon noticed his thoughts: I have to do it all. I had to drive Tevi to the doctor and wait there. Now I have to wait here. When he heard the "have to" messages he had been giving himself, he decided to change his mind. *I get to*, he chose to tell himself. I get to make sure my son gets the health care he needs. I get to show him I care enough to drive all over town. I get to be with my boy while he is sick.

When Brandon changed his mind by changing how he talked about his current circumstance, he stopped resisting it. By emotionally accepting his present parenting moment, he was able to relax. He even smiled to himself as he thought, I'm glad I get to be here with my son and help him get well. I'll bet a lot of fathers miss this special time.

*****

"John, you have to come home right away!" Those were the words John Fulton heard when he took a call from his wife, Judy, one

afternoon in his real estate office. Her tone and words revealed more that a hint of panic.

"Is everything OK? Are you all right?" he inquired.

"I'm fine," Judy responded, "but everything isn't OK. It's Aaron. He shoplifted. This is awful. I'm so embarrassed. I don't know what to do. This is terrible!"

"Just take some deep breaths, Judy. Let me hear you breathe."

"He had four candy bars in his pocket when we got home from the grocery store. I confronted him and he confessed that he just helped himself. What are we going to do? I'm so upset! John—our son shoplifted!"

"You sound really frustrated and it seems like you aren't sure what to do."

"Well, what can I do, John? He just takes things off the shelves and stuffs them in his pockets. I want you to come home right now and help me deal with this. This is a real crisis!"

"I'll leave in three minutes. And one thing I want you to do before I get home is change your mind about this."

"What do you mean?"

"You keep saying this is awful. I think it would be helpful if we saw it as perfect."

"I don't think you understand. Your son SHOPLIFTED!"

"Yes, I know. And we can do a better job of helping him if we see this as perfect. Eight years old really is the perfect time to learn about taking other people's belongings without asking or paying for them. Better now than at eighteen if he helps himself to someone's car."

"John, I don't think you realize how serious this is."

"Honey, I do believe this is very serious. And I'm also serious about this being the perfect time to help Aaron learn an important lesson. I'll be there in ten minutes. I'm heading out the door right now. Bye."

John and his wife huddled in their living room for an hour

discussing the situation and planning what to do about their son and the candy bar caper. Together, they devised the following plan.

1. They called the store owner and told him what had happened. They told him they would be bringing their son in to make amends.
2. They solicited the store owner's cooperation. They asked him to be serious and explain to the boy what happens when shoplifters are caught, but not to go overboard. The store owner agreed.
3. They helped their son construct a verbal message to make amends with the store owner. They taught him to tell what he had learned from the experience and what he intended to do differently next time.
4. The parents accompanied their son to the store to show support for him and the store owner.

The incident turned out to be a wonderful learning experience for everyone. The young son learned what happens when you take things from a store without paying. He also learned how to make amends when you make a mistake. His parents learned the value of managing their minds before they managed the situation.

*****

Maria wasn't surprised when she learned that her son had been diagnosed with dyslexia. Pedro had been having trouble with reading since first grade. She knew something was amiss, but she didn't know exactly what was causing his frustration. Now that the tests had given his condition a name, Maria assumed a stance of calm determination. She turned immediately to the serenity prayer in an effort to manage her own mind before she attempted to manage the new situation.

Grant me the serenity to accept the things I cannot change, the courage to change the things I can, and the wisdom to know the difference.

Maria did not simply recite the serenity prayer. She put it to work in her life by using it to manage her mind. She knew she could not change her son's condition, but what she could do was learn more about it and help Pedro compensate for it and work to overcome it. The prayer helped her remember that time invested in wishing and hoping things would be different would be time not spent in dealing with the situation at hand.

Because of the prayer and her willingness to put it to use in her life, Maria was able to determine what she could and could not change. She took responsibility for her choices and was able to let go of the rest. Her choice of how to manage her mind helped her stay calm as well as determined.

*****

The Wilson family was going on a family vacation. Their destination, a small lake in northern Michigan, was a five-hour car ride away—not an easy trip with Madison, their four-year-old daughter, and Justin, their five-year-old son.

Hank and Meredith Wilson were well prepared for the journey. They had put together individual car packs designed to keep the preschoolers occupied during the long ride with books, games, crayons, paper, cars, dolls, snacks, and surprises.

Ten minutes into the journey, the road angled sharply to the left. The centrifugal force generated by the abrupt turn of the car caused Madison to cross the imaginary line in the center of the back seat. Her brother immediately poked her, provoking a silent shoving match. Their mother gave them both a loving smile and they settled down.

Twenty minutes later, Madison dropped a crayon and it rolled under Justin's feet. As she reached to get it, she brushed Justin's shoe. He kicked in retaliation and a light tussle ensued. Mrs. Wilson responded by telling the children that their dad drove best in a stress-free environment and reminding them to respect each other's space. They did—for a while.

Ninety minutes into the trip, both children contracted a case of the sillies. While their giggling was cute at first, it persisted to the point of annoyance. Although they were asked to choose a different behavior, the giggling continued.

Hank could feel his anger mounting. The giggling was breaking his concentration, and the heavy amount of traffic heading north on a Friday night required 100 percent of his attention. He started to issue a direct order and then stopped.

These kids are just being five, he reasoned, speaking to himself before he spoke to his children. Giggling and wiggling is what four and five year olds do, he thought to himself. Getting mad at them for giggling would be like getting mad at a dog for barking. Dogs bark. Cats meow. And four and five year olds giggle and wiggle.

Hank pulled the car into the next rest stop and turned off the engine. "Everyone out," he announced. "Race you to the picnic table." The race led to a game of tag, which turned into hide-and-seek, which evolved into wrestling in the leaves. The entire episode took fifteen minutes.

When the car swung back onto the highway, Hank's children were calm and relaxed. So was he. The sillies had disappeared and been replaced by quiet attentiveness to the story Meredith was now reading.

Because Hank was able to manage his own mind before he attempted to manage his children, he created a successful beginning for the family vacation.

Managing Your Mind Challenge

How are you doing with managing your mind first? Read through the items below. They are intended to help you take stock of where you are now on implementing the fourth commitment. Rate yourself on each issue. Use this challenge to determine areas you would like to improve, continue as is, or celebrate as successful.

Time Out

How do you pause to manage your own mind? Do you take three deep breaths, count to ten, or go for a short walk if necessary? Do you call for a time out so you can move UP before you move IN?

Self-Talk

To what degree do you monitor your self-talk? What do you tell yourself concerning your children? Do you use self-talk purposefully to create a desired result in your family?

Vision

Before you move IN, can you expand your vision to see more in this child than his or her current behavior? Will you remember that he is more than his report card, that she is more than the act she is choosing at this moment?

Strength Searching

Can you see strengths in your child's current misbehavior? What is it about this behavior that, if it occurred in a different setting, would be positive?

Help

How would it change your parenting if you chose thoughts that allowed you to interpret misbehavior as a call for help rather than as misbehavior? In what ways would your responses to those behaviors be altered?

Crisis

Can you see this present crisis as a learning process? Would that make the crisis wonderful, exciting, beneficial, necessary, terrible, or something else? Are you not responsible for how you see this crisis?

Remembering

As you struggle with your child today, ask yourself, Is there something I have forgotten? What is it that I am not remembering here?

Beginner's Eyes

Look at your child today with beginner's eyes. See everything as if you were seeing it for the first time. Pretend you and your child are new to each other. What would you see if you saw with beginner's eyes?

Miracles

Somewhere today you could create a miracle by shifting your perception. Will you notice it? Will you make the shift?

Wounded

What if you saw this child as wounded rather than as wrong? Would it alter your approach? Would it change your attitude?

Bigger

Instead of working to make your parenting problem smaller, why not strive to become bigger than the problem? Can you rise above it by turning your binoculars around and looking through the lens that make the problem look smaller?

Attitude

As you implement consequences today, what if you concentrate not on what you are doing but on the attitude with which you are doing it?

Acceptance

What if all your efforts to help this child will be worth nothing until you emotionally accept her the way she is? Can you do that?

Release

What if this particular situation with this particular child had to surface before it could be worked through and released? Maybe this situation is the most important thing that will happen to her this year. Maybe it is no accident that it surfaced in your presence. Can you help her to work it through?

Open Mind

What parenting solution is failing to find you today because you assume you already have it?

Conclusion

Managing your mind is no more difficult than managing your wardrobe or your hair as you get dressed in the morning. Beginning to take charge of this important parenting commitment requires only that you create a place for it on your list of priorities.

Once you commit to managing your mind by moving UP in your consciousness before you move IN with your actions, it becomes necessary to stay conscious of your parenting thoughts. You must make a decision to be alert and monitor your thoughts to see if they're leading you in the direction of creating yourself as the parent you truly want to be.

You must also stay aware of your actions. Are they congruent with your personal parenting vision? Do they resonate with the principles you say you live by? If not, use the mind skills detailed in this chapter to parent your children in the way you wanted to be parented as a child.

Your frame if mind is too important to leave to chance. Take charge. Manage your mind first by moving UP in your consciousness before you move IN with your actions.

The Fifth Commitment

I commit to focusing on the search for solutions.

I realize that fixing the problem is more important than fixing blame. I pledge to invest my time and effort in seeking solutions rather than in blame and punishment. I search for solutions.

Imagine your child bursting through the front door to tell you his sister has just been hit by a car in front of your home. You rush to the scene and find her with a broken leg, cuts, and assorted bruises. Would you launch into an immediate investigation to find out whose fault it was? Would you invest your time in collecting several versions of the accident so you could blame those you determined to be responsible?

Hardly! You would take action by calling for an ambulance, covering your daughter with a blanket, and offering reassurance. Any time spent fixing blame, in your mind or aloud, would delay getting medical attention for your child and providing parental comfort.

Blame and faultfinding serve no useful purpose in an emergency—and they serve no useful purpose in our everyday parenting lives, either. Energy spent blaming your son for spilling milk does not improve his milk-pouring skills for next time. Angrily reprimanding your daughter for forgetting to feed the dog does not insure that the dog will be fed tomorrow. Finding fault with your teen's decision to come home late does nothing to move the two of you toward finding a workable solution.

You have a limited amount of parenting time available to you. Any time you invest in finding fault, distributing blame, and handing out punishments is time that is not available for searching for solutions or altering the situation.

A commitment to search for solutions begins with the adult. Before involving your child in the solution-seeking process, look at the problem to determine what parenting move would be most helpful to him or her. As a parent, you have two basic options available to you in dealing with behavioral problems. You can move to correct a behavior with either "structure" or "nurture." A structural move would be one that establishes a routine, changes a schedule, or sets a limit. A nurturing move would involve consoling, providing support, offering assistance, or creating space for your child to learn. Those are your two basic choices.

When Martha's three-year-old son, Anthony, began biting other children at day care, she noticed that the onset of the biting coincided with a change in the visitation schedule with his father, who had recently remarried. At the time of his father's marriage, Anthony's overnight stays with his dad increased to every other night during the week. Martha discussed this with her ex-husband and the two decided to group their son's overnight stays to create a long weekend visit rather than maintaining an every-other-night schedule. When they implemented the change in structure, the biting episodes subsided.

Arthur's teenage son, Rob, had been skipping basketball practice and demonstrating aggressive behavior in games on the court. After numerous calls from the coach regarding Rob's behavior, Arthur met his son after school one day and the two went out for a bite to eat before practice. Through the conversation that took place over their meal, Arthur learned that when his son forgot his practice jersey the coach made him play in a shirt that had printed on the back: I FORGOT MY JERSEY. I'M A MORON. When Rob told the coach how he felt when he was treated that way, the coach told him to

stop his whining and quit acting like a baby. Rob felt angry and disempowered. His desire to play basketball was being overshadowed by his feelings of hurt and anger.

Rob skipped basketball practice that day and, with the assistance of his father, drafted a letter to the school's athletic director. Arthur guided his son through the process of filing a complaint and expressing his feelings appropriately. A meeting was scheduled between the coach, the athletic director, Rob, and Arthur. At the meeting, they discussed many issues, including the behavior of both Rob and the coach. Rob decided to finish the season and remain a part of the basketball team. Arthur remained in close contact with the coach and together they tracked Rob's progress through the rest of the season. Arthur's choice of the nurture option in dealing with his son helped Rob find an appropriate solution.

Many children have learned to deny, disown, and discount problems, sweeping them under the rug and pretending they don't exist. What these children need is a model of an adult who is committed to searching for solutions when problems arise. An integral part of this commitment involves teaching your children a solution-seeking process and using that process yourself.

If your child spills milk three days in a row at the dinner table, you have a problem. Blaming, faultfinding, and punishing won't solve it. Nor will your choice of those behaviors model a mature approach to searching for solutions. Get the milk cleaned up. Involve your child if he or she is old enough. Later, when the minor crisis is over, guide your son or daughter through a solution-seeking process aimed at ending the problem (spilled milk) by coming up with a workable solution.

Begin by seeing the problem as an opportunity. Seeing a problem as an opportunity is the first step in searching for a solution. In this case, spilled milk is an opportunity to teach your child how to handle milk without spilling it and to model how to handle problems effectively.

Next, define the problem: *Milk is getting spilled regularly and it ruins the carpet. We need to find a way to keep it from being spilled.* Now invite your child to join you in brainstorming possible solutions to the stated problem. This is not the time to evaluate proposed solutions. Simply list them.

Possible solutions to the milk-spilling problem might include:

- Practice pouring milk over the sink.
- Keep milk glasses away from the edge of the table.
- Put a plastic sheet down on the rug.
- Fill milk glasses only halfway.
- Have nothing else in your hands as you reach for the milk.

After the list has been completed, talk about the proposed solutions until everyone involved agrees on which one, or which combination, should be implemented.

Once you've arrived at a consensus, make a commitment to the solution you've agreed to try. Check back a few days later at a preset time to evaluate. At that point, either go back to the drawing board or keep implementing the successful solution.

The solution-seeking process can be summarized as follows:

1. See the problem as an opportunity.
2. Define the problem.
3. Brainstorm possible solutions.
4. Reach consensus.
5. Commit.
6. Set a date to evaluate.
7. Evaluate.

When moving through the solution-seeking process with your child, remember that the process is more important than the product. It matters less what specific solution is proposed and more that you

74

go through the appropriate process to produce it. The goal is to help your children learn and become comfortable with the process of finding solutions so they can apply the process to future problems they encounter.

Solution seeking takes time. Yes, it is quicker simply to tell your children what to do. Yes, it is easier to come up with a solution yourself and require that it be implemented. Clearly, it is more efficient to do it yourself. But *efficient* does not always equate with *effective*. It is more effective in the long run to involve your children in the search for solutions. It is more effective to have them experience the solution-seeking process than to merely tell them how to solve their problems. If raising competent, caring, confident children is your goal, think in terms of being effective, not of being efficient.

As you teach your children how to be effective solution seekers, remember that children are not always in a solution-seeking mode. When your son is crying because juice was spilled on the picture he drew and left on the table, he is not emotionally ready to engage in solution seeking at that moment. When your daughter is distraught because she needs the computer to finish her homework and her brother is using it to play games, it's premature and counterproductive to begin immediately searching for solutions. An important role of parents is to help a child get into a frame of mind that fosters solution seeking before they begin searching for solutions to the problem at hand.

Solution seeking and problem solving take place in an area of the brain called the frontal lobe. This area is the output and control center for behavior. The frontal lobe helps an individual create choices, choose among options, compare possible outcomes, and manage behavior. Be assured that when your daughter is throwing a tantrum she is not using her frontal lobe. Nor is your son using his frontal lobe when he's yelling, "I hate you."

When your child demonstrates physical behavior such as hitting,

kicking, biting, throwing objects, stomping feet, and swinging arms, he or she is in tantrum mode. Such behavior is generated in the midbrain, not in the cortex, where the frontal lobe is located. Yelling, screaming, crying, and other emotional behaviors are generated in the limbic brain, which assists in managing emotional content and is not typically a problem-solving area.

As a parent, it's important that you recognize these behaviors and understand that your child is not in an appropriate space from which to engage in or accept problem-solving strategies. Attempting to problem solve in the middle of a tantrum or during an emotional outburst will serve no useful purpose. Your role at this time is to help your child pass through the tantrum phase and move into a problem-solving mode.

To move a child into his frontal lobe and thus into a space conducive to problem solving, calmly use words to paint a picture of the behaviors or emotions that you observe. If your son is having a tantrum, say, "Your legs are kicking. Your arms are swinging around. Your teeth are clenched and your body is moving all over the place." If your daughter storms out of the computer room slamming the door and announcing how unfair the world is, tell her, "I hear anger in your voice. You seem frustrated. The sound of the door slamming shook the whole house." This type of parental response helps children to identify and recognize their own behavior and emotion. As they do this, they become aware of themselves, and the frontal lobe becomes activated.

Follow your words by allowing the child several minutes of solitude in a calming place. The brain will slowly shift into higher cortical thinking and frontal lobe activation. When you and your child have made this transition, the solution-seeking process is ready to begin.

Some individuals move into the solution-seeking mode faster than others do. For some children it could require only seconds, while for others it may take up to 30 minutes. Give your child what-

ever time he or she needs to get ready and the solution-seeking process will be more productive and rewarding for both of you.

Life Examples

Mary Jenkins is a single mom who gets up and off to work before the sun comes up. She wakes her boys, ages 11 and 9, before she leaves. They fix breakfast on their own and take the bus to school.

Recently, the boys had been going back to sleep after their mom left. Their goal was to grab a few more precious moments in bed before they began their day. As a result, twice in one week the boys overslept and missed the bus. Consequently, they also missed school.

Mary knew that any form of punishment she could devise would only be a short-term solution. She wanted more than that. She wanted the problem fixed and fixed permanently so that she could go off to work without worrying about whether or not her children would get on the bus.

Mary thought about calling the boys from work each morning to make sure they were up and moving but rejected that idea because it didn't help them become responsible for getting themselves up and to school on time. She wanted a solution that put the responsibility in her children's hands while simultaneously giving her peace of mind.

On Sunday afternoon, Mary and the boys discussed ways to make sure the children met the 7:30 a.m. bus on a regular basis. After a brief discussion, a decision was made to purchase two alarm clocks, one for each child. Mary invested time teaching the boys how to set the alarms and watched as they each practiced several times. The three of them agreed to implement this solution for one week and then get back together to discuss its effectiveness.

The following Sunday afternoon Mary and her boys came together to evaluate. Since the children had arrived at the bus stop on time each day during the preceding week, they used the Sunday

meeting time to celebrate their success. Because of their efforts, they now have a picture of themselves as a family group who can successfully search for and find solutions to their problems.

*****

The Wilsons, the McGregors, the Gonzalezes, the Cartwrights, and the Schmitts had something in common. Each couple had a young son who wouldn't go to bed at night without a struggle. Each set of parents was frustrated and unsure of what to do, but they were all committed to finding a solution.

After thinking and talking about the problem, the Wilsons decided to create a bedtime routine, a consistent ritual they would practice every evening. Their ritual included a ten-minute warning, dirty clothes in the hamper, bath, pajamas, teeth brushing, stories, prayers, hugs, and kisses. Since they repeated the routine with consistency, the parents and the child began to rely on it. It provided structure and security. Everyone knew and could anticipate what would happen next. As use of the structure became habit, the bedtime resistance decreased.

Tina and Steve McGregor also engaged in solution seeking. What does this child really need? they asked themselves. What is he trying to get? What does he want to accomplish? They determined that their son, Max, was afraid and needed to feel safe. "What would help you feel safer?" they asked their three-year-old. After listening carefully to his answers, they explained to him that one of their main jobs was to help him feel safe. Together they created a plan that included leaving the door open and using a friendly teddy bear to increase Max's feelings of security. They also began "brooming out" all the monsters as part of the regular bedtime ritual. When the monsters disappeared, Max's feeling of safety returned.

Ivonne and Alec Gonzalez determined that their son, Felipe, was resisting bedtime because he wanted in on the action. Exciting

things were going on downstairs and he wanted to be a part of them. He didn't want to miss out on any of the good stuff. Their diagnosis called for a different bedtime prescription. They decided to make sure the "good stuff" wasn't that good. At bedtime, they turned off the TV and engaged in quiet activities. When Felipe appeared, they explained to him that when he goes to bed, it's time for them to get their work done. They invited him to join in folding laundry, doing dishes, and sweeping the kitchen floor. When their youngster realized that the adult agenda wasn't fun, the bedtime hassle diminished significantly.

The Cartwrights hypothesized that their child was resisting bedtime because he wasn't tired yet. They discussed possible solutions, including setting a later bedtime, eliminating his afternoon nap, or getting him up earlier in the morning. They decided it would be much easier to wake their son up than get him to sleep. Consequently, their plan centered on an earlier wakeup call.

The Schmitts' son, Luke, got out of bed because he wanted a drink. To solve their bedtime resistance problem, his parents added a drink to the regular nighttime routine. They also provided a special cup that stayed in Luke's room. If he got thirsty during the night, he could use the cup to get a drink and then go directly back to bed.

Each couple created a solution based on their personal observations of the problem. Each chose to search for a solution rather than to blame and punish. Each created an effective solution based on love, respect, and the belief that every problem has a solution.

*****

Tonya and Ray regularly walked their three-year-old son, Michael, down the driveway to get the mail. Their home was located on a narrow, busy country road where cars reached speeds of 50-55 miles per hour or more. The mailbox was on the other side of this potentially dangerous road.

The regular mail-collecting ritual was simple and safe. As the family reached the road, one parent would stay behind and hold Michael's hand. The other parent modeled crossing the street safely by looking both ways several times, waiting patiently for all the cars to pass, and staying focused on the task.

One day, as Tonya started across the street, Michael began to scream, "I want to get the mail! I want to get the mail!" and tried to pull away from his father. Ray held firmly to his son's hand and said, "No. It's not safe. Mom will get it and bring it back to us."

Michael threw his body to the ground kicking and screaming. Ray bent down next to his son and said, "You look frustrated. You want to cross the street and get the mail and I won't let you. Your whole body is showing your anger and your voice is loud. You're angry." Michael kept on kicking and screaming. Quietly, Ray continued to describe the situation. "I wonder if the people in the cars can hear you as they zoom past. Look, there goes one now. Wow! That was fast."

Michael looked up.

Looking up was the signal Ray was watching for. When he observed the slight change in his son's behavior, he quickly picked him up and said, "Michael, I want to keep you safe, and you want to get the mail. Let's go back to the house with Mom, and the three of us will talk about all the ways you can get the mail safely."

Once back at the house, Tonya and Ray talked about the cars on the road and how fast they go. They talked about how difficult it is to see people on the road as they zoom past. They agreed with Michael that he should be able to have a turn to get the mail, and together they brainstormed ideas about how to do that safely.

Michael suggested moving the mailbox. Dad suggested driving up to the mailbox in the car. Mom suggested carrying Michael in her arms as Dad watched closely for cars. With a little guidance and a lot of respect for each other's opinions, Michael chose Mom's idea. With a clear plan articulated and a promise that it would be

implemented the next day, Michael smiled and happily ran into the next room to play.

As Michael grew in size and experience, the family revisited the mailbox issue occasionally to explore other safe ways to get the mail. Each time, Michael was an integral part of the decision-making process, and each time he left the discussion with a smile on his face. He felt included, important, and empowered. And he was learning the important life skill of solution seeking.

*****

Brandon is an eleven-year-old bed wetter. If his bed is wet in the morning, he finds himself the target of verbal anger, usually delivered by his father, whose intention is to shame Brandon into new behavior. The shaming is not working, but his parents persist. They don't know what else to do so they direct their energy toward their son rather than toward creating a solution.

A.J. is also an eleven-year-old bed wetter. His parents have been to their family doctor in an effort to search for solutions. From the doctor they learned that many boys continue to wet the bed into their teen years. The doctor suggested a ban on drinking anything after 6:00 p.m. and a more relaxed attitude on the part of the parents.

When A.J.'s parents got home from the doctor's office, they held a family meeting. They asked A.J. if he wanted to stay dry during the night or if he wanted to maintain the status quo. He said he wanted to learn to stay dry.

With the help of his mother and father, A.J. created a plan to take responsibility for his bedwetting. The plan included no drinks after 6:00 p.m. and a full emptying of his bladder before bedtime. Using his alarm clock, he gets up once a night, at 1:30 a.m., to empty his bladder again. If his bedding and pajamas are wet in the morning, he immediately takes them to the laundry room and puts them into the washing machine so they're ready for the dryer when he gets home

from school. It's his responsibility to transfer them and be sure they're dry and ready to go back on his bed before bedtime.

While A.J.'s parents monitor their son's behavior to see if the plan is working, they refrain from engaging in lectures or reprimands.

*****

At four years of age, Timmy was quite a painter. He would stand at the easel for hours mixing colors onto a big sheet of white paper. His imagination soared as he talked about his creations in the making.

It should come as no surprise that Timmy also made quite a mess while he painted. Tempera paint was spilled across the floor. Paint dripped from the bottom of the easel. Timmy himself was often the recipient of errant brush strokes. He got paint on his hands, smock, and face.

Yet, when the easel had been put away and the room was being used for other activities later in the day, no one could tell that paint had adorned the floor a short time ago. No clue was left to suggest that painting had occurred at all.

The clean room, the dried easel, and the freshly scrubbed budding artist were not accidental. Nor were they a one-time occurrence. From the very first moment Timmy showed an interest in painting, his mother helped him learn the process of cleaning up spills. When a spill occurred, there was no yelling, no chastising, and no issuing of orders. Instead, Timmy's mother would say, "Oh, a spill. What could we do about that? What could we use to clean that up?" She would then help him clean it up and encourage him to continue painting.

Occasionally, Timmy's mother redirected him by asking questions like, "Where could we put the paint to avoid another spill?" "Would it be easier for you if the paint was in a different container?" "What could we put on the floor so paint won't stain the floor?" She spent

a lot of time helping Timmy discover the answers to these and similar questions.

At an early age, Timmy was encouraged and challenged to think through the spilled paint problem and come up with solutions. Now, at age four, he was taking care of the paint setup and cleanup mostly by himself. The assistance he required was minimal. By investing the time to practice solution seeking with her son, Timmy's mother had made herself dispensable and her son more independent.

*****

Bradley's father was a problem solver. If something broke, he fixed it. If a problem surfaced, he solved it. If an answer was needed, he supplied it. Problems didn't last long at Bradley's house. His father saw to that. He was skillful, efficient, and thorough in his problem solving.

Although at first glance Bradley's father appeared to be a great model for solution seeking, a closer look revealed a different picture.

Bradley's father was a quiet man. When he went after a solution, he didn't say much about what he was doing or why. He simply took action without articulating any of the thoughts that went on in his mind. One day, Bradley's mother couldn't get the top-right-hand drawer of the antique desk open. She asked her husband for help. Bradley's father looked at it for a few minutes, yanked on it, and then opened up the top drawer on the left side. That action unlocked the right-hand drawer.

Bradley was impressed. The action reaffirmed a belief he had been cultivating for several years: *When you're an adult, you know*. A corollary belief was that, until then, you wouldn't be able to solve much because you're only a child. He could look forward to being an adult because *adults know*.

What Bradley missed learning from his father was the lengthy and creative thinking that went on in his mind as he figured out how

to tackle a problem. In dealing with the stuck drawer, his father mentally went through a series of possible solutions. He originally thought he could force it open and tried that, but to no avail. He thought about kicking it, but rejected that idea since he was wearing only socks on his feet. He thought about getting a screwdriver and forcing it between the top of the desk and the top of the drawer and wiggling it back and forth. He dismissed that idea because it might leave marks on the wood of this beautiful antique. That's when Bradley's father guessed that the drawer that appeared to be stuck had a catch on it that would be released by opening another drawer.

Since Bradley was unaware of the solution-seeking process that went on in his father's head, he just figured, When you're an adult, you know.

Search for Solutions Challenge

Do you regularly search for solutions? Do you help your children learn and use a problem-solving process? Where do you stand in relation to the fifth commitment? Check below to determine areas of strength and places that could use improvement. Set some parenting goals as you challenge yourself to look closely at the issue of solution seeking.

Perception

Do you see problems as an opportunity or as a hassle? Do you enjoy helping your children search for solutions, or do you see their problems as an invasion of your personal time? How do you typically perceive problems? Be assured that your perception will affect your attitude and your behaviors.

Attitude

Do you enjoy seeking solutions with your children, or do you dread it? When a parenting problem surfaces, is your first reaction one of frustration, or do you look to the situation with anticipation? Are you able to choose your attitude when a solution is needed, or do you just accept whatever attitude shows up?

Involvement

Are you willing to guide, direct, explore, and discover solutions in a partnership with your children? Will you remain invested in only what you want to have happen, or are there times when you can allow a different lesson to be learned?

Time

Do you take the time to help your children come to their own conclusion, or are you more likely to provide one for them? Will you let them struggle with an issue and encourage them to stay focused on the process of discovering answers? Will you allow a solution to take shape, or will you force it to unfold? Will you think in terms of the quick fix, or will you invest time in helping your child search for solutions?

Modeling

Do you let your children see you struggle with a problem? Do you let them see you make a mistake and then change your approach? Will you problem solve aloud so they can become aware of your thought processes? Will you ask them for help and include them in brainstorming a problem you are having?

Readiness

Will you say, "Give me a moment. I need to calm my mind so I can get in a solution-seeking mode"? When you're angry or sad do you give yourself the time and space to deal with your emotions, or do you stuff your feelings and push for an immediate decision on what to do about a problem?

Process vs. Product

Are you quick to jump to the solution you prefer, or are you committed to involving your children in the search for solutions? Do you have faith that a solution-seeking process will result in finding workable solutions? Can you allow your children to implement a solution you believe is unworkable to see if it will work? If the solution does not work, will you teach your children how to go back to the drawing board and create a new solution?

Interpersonal Problems

Are you comfortable inviting your children to search for solutions to interpersonal problems? Can you suspend your need to be right and invest more time in listening than in telling? Can you react nondefensively if you are identified as part of the problem?

Beliefs

Do you believe that if you want a behavior you need to teach a behavior? Do you believe that the time invested in solution seeking is worthwhile or that it is more efficient to tell children what to do? Do you believe that attaching blame and finding fault is part of your role as a parent? Do you believe that how you approach solving problems influences how your children approach similar situations?

Conclusion

Committing to search for solutions means that you commit to focusing on the process of helping your children learn how to search for solutions rather than relying on punishment to teach the lesson.

Your commitment to search for solutions empowers your children. It helps them see themselves as part of a powerful solution-seeking team, your primary family unit. In addition, it helps them see themselves as solution-seeking individuals in their own right.

The Sixth Commitment

I commit to speaking self-responsible language.

My language patterns reflect my belief in autonomy, personal responsibility, and ownership of one's actions and feelings. I learn and use language that helps my children see themselves as cause. I speak self-responsible language.

Self-responsible language consists of words and phrases that reveal an acceptance of responsibility for one's actions and feelings, show ownership for results, or make choices conscious. Examples include:

"I'm creating a lot of irritation about this situation." (Shows responsibility for one's feelings.)

"My response helped create this situation." (Shows ownership for results.)

"I'm choosing to stay away from you right now." (Makes choices conscious.)

Language that is not self-responsible consists of words and phrases that deny responsibility for one's actions and feelings, blame someone or something else, or keep choices unconscious. Examples include:

"She irritated the heck out of me." (Blames someone else.)

"It wasn't my fault." (Denies responsibility for one's actions.)

"It just came over me. I didn't know what I was doing." (Keeps choices unconscious.)

There is a powerful theme running through his chapter. Put simply: *There is a connection between the words you use, the beliefs you hold, and the actions you take.* Yes, we are suggesting

that your language patterns influence your behaviors.

Consider the parent whose language is full of "makes me" verbal responses.

"Noisy children *irritate me*."

"Gum chewing *annoys me*."

"You *tick me off* when you talk like that."

When you repeatedly use "makes me" talk, you reinforce the belief that others can indeed make you feel a feeling or take an action. In truth, no one can make you feel or do anything. No one can make you mad without your consent. In fact, someone can be actively *trying* to make you mad, and if you don't buy in, their efforts lead nowhere.

When you believe that others can "make you" feel something, your behaviors flow from that belief. You are less likely to take responsibility for your own feelings and actions when you assume a victim stance and blame others for your choices.

The mother who believes that noisy children annoy her reacts differently to noise than the mother who believes annoyance is a feeling she may or may not choose in response to noise. The father who believes that his child "made me" spank him disowns responsibility for his actions and blames his own hitting behavior on the child's hitting of his brother. The parent who believes rainy days drive her crazy is less empowered and perceives less choice in her life than the parent who believes that rainy days are simply rainy days and that they have no power to drive anyone anywhere.

The commitment to use self-responsible language calls upon you to remove from your vocabulary words and phrases that point to others as the cause of your choices and behavior. Many people, children and adults alike, simply don't realize that they choose their own attitudes and behaviors. They firmly believe someone or something else is responsible for their actions, and their language reflects that belief. They say things like . . .

"That depresses me."

"You kids make me angry."

"He hurt my feelings."

"She made me do it."

The words you use when you speak to yourself or your children begin to create a mindset. Your words give structure to your thoughts. Repetitious thought influences the beliefs you hold, and your actions flow from your belief system. Language that is not self-responsible, repeated often enough, creates beliefs that others can *make you* feel and act in certain ways. You begin to believe that you are not the cause of your attitudes and behaviors and that someone or something else is.

We recently did a series of parenting seminars in Mexico. While there, we made an interesting discovery. All the young children in Mexico speak Spanish! It's amazing. By three or four years of age, these children are already speaking a foreign language!

Of course they speak Spanish, and we all know why. They speak Spanish because Spanish is spoken in the home. They are immersed in it day in and day out. The children learn it quickly and easily.

Similarly, children raised in homes where language that reflects a lack of self-responsibility predominates grow up speaking that language. They consistently choose language patterns that disown responsibility for their behaviors and feelings, deny choice, and portray them as victims. Because that's the language they speak, that's the way they behave. They act irresponsibly, easily assume a victim position, and behave as if they have no choice. Their behavior springs from beliefs that were developed through repetitious use of the language they have consistently heard spoken and now mimic.

Please make a commitment to teach your child a "foreign" language—the language of responsibility. Children deserve to have self-responsible language spoken in their homes. They deserve to have it consistently modeled for them, and they deserve to be taught how to use it themselves. When you teach children to speak and

think self-responsibly, you increase the odds that they will act self-responsibly.

One effective way of changing "makes me" language is to change the word that immediately precedes "makes me" to "I." "*You* make me so angry" then becomes "*I* make me so angry." "That depresses me" becomes "I'm depressed." This may sound awkward at first. "I made myself angry," "I make me frustrated," and "I made myself jealous" are certainly not common phrases. But the technique puts you in charge of your feelings and actions and helps keep the focus on the real power you have. Model it for your children often so they become familiar with the sounds of self-responsible speech.

Another way of speaking that leaves you clearly in control of your responses is to use the phrase "I'm choosing." "I'm choosing to be mad," "I chose embarrassment when he said that," and "Right now I'm choosing anger" are all examples of this technique. By choosing such phrases, you remind yourself of the role you play in activating your emotional responses. You bring your choices to a conscious level and you increase your options and your sense of personal power. It is another effective way to model self-responsible speaking for your children.

Teach these techniques to your children directly. Do not accept "makes me" language in your home. Language that places blame on adults, peers, siblings, or some other external force is inappropriate. Help children learn to restate their "makes me" language. When your daughter says, "He made me do it," say to her, "You mean *you chose* to do it. Go ahead and say that. Say, 'I chose to do it.'" When your teenage son gives you an angry look and says, "You make me so mad," say to him, "You are mad *and* you have power over that feeling. I don't have power over your feelings. It's OK to just say, 'I'm mad.' You get to be mad at me and still be in control of your feelings."

Another component of self-responsible language is that of

making choice conscious. Use the words "choose" and "decide" to model this concept and help your children become conscious of their choices.

"I'm choosing to get started right away."

"I've decided to save this for later."

"When you choose to throw the trucks, you also choose to play without them for a while."

Implementing the sixth commitment also calls upon you to drop "I can't" from your verbal repertoire. "I can't" is a self-limiting phrase that disowns responsibility for the decisions that you make. It is a way of denying personal responsibility. "I can't get my kids to behave at the grocery store," "I can't think of anything else to do," "I can't get my son to come home on time," "I can't quit smoking" are phrases that deny personal responsibility. These "I can't" phrases and others like them have no place in a home where self-responsible language is the goal.

Replace your "I can't" language with "I don't," "I won't," or "I choose not to." If you say, "I *don't* get my kids to behave at the grocery store," you no longer disown responsibility but open the door to exploring new approaches and learning new skills in behavior management. Saying "I *won't* think of anything else to do" is being truthful about the situation at that very moment. You can then choose to think of something else to do in a later moment. Saying, "I *choose not to* quit smoking" acknowledges your power over the smoking habit, and when you choose to quit, the task will be easier to accomplish.

Using self-responsible language demonstrates integrity. When you behave with integrity, you say what you are going to do and then do what you say. When your actions support your words, other people, including your children, learn that what you say you mean—that your word can be trusted.

Children learn about integrity by watching and listening to the adults around them. When Dad says, "I'll read you that story later,"

and then doesn't follow through, his child learns that Dad's words can't be trusted. When Mom says, "No, we are not buying a toy at the store today," and then gives in when her daughter continues to whine, the child witnesses her mother's lack of integrity. When children observe their parents' lack of integrity, they learn that they don't have to match their behavior to their words either.

Conversely, children learn integrity when they see their parents' behavior aligning with their words. When you say to your child, "We don't use those kinds of words in our house," and those kinds of words are in fact not used, you model integrity. If you say to your son, "The next time you leave your bike in the middle of the driveway you'll lose the opportunity to ride it," and he sees you hanging his bike on a hook in the garage when you find it in the driveway again the next evening, your words have meaning. When you say to your daughter, "I'll pick you up at five," and you're there at five to pick her up, you demonstrate the use of self-responsible language.

Encourage your children to think through their choices and options, pick one, and state it verbally. Then guide them toward the behavior that reflects the option they chose. In this way you teach them how to say what they are going to do and how to do what they say. You teach integrity.

By intentionally selecting words and phrases that demonstrate integrity and encourage self-responsibility, you empower your children and enhance their effectiveness as capable, caring human beings.

Life Examples

During a recent family therapy session, 15-year-old Michael started yelling at his parents. "You're so controlling. You tell me everything to do. You won't let me make any decision for myself. You make me so angry." Several times during his venting, he repeated, "You make me so angry."

The family therapist stopped Michael at the end of one of his "You

make me so angry" statements and asked, "Michael, are you sure you want to give your parents all that power over your feelings?"

"Well, it's their fault I feel this way," Michael snapped.

"Life's easier that way, isn't it?" replied the therapist.

"No, it's not," Michael retorted. "Life sucks around them. They keep me down!"

The therapist looked at Michael and calmly said, "Michael, you're giving your parents power over the one thing you can control: your feelings. It may be true that your parents are controlling and make many decisions for you," he continued, "but you don't have to give them control over your feelings. No one can make you feel a certain way unless you relinquish the control of your feelings to them."

"I'm not sure I get what you mean." Michael looked puzzled.

The therapist went on, "What if you started saying to your parents, 'I'm angry when you don't involve me in decisions that affect me?' How do you think they would respond?"

Michael sat quietly for a moment, then said, "I don't know."

"Well, pick one of those things you're angry about and state it to them the way I suggested."

Michael turned to his parents and said, "I'm angry that you made me take Advanced English and never asked me what I thought. I got a D in the class the first marking period and then you guys grounded me because I got such a bad grade."

"You got a bad grade because you refused to work in the class," Michael's father told his son.

"I refused to work because I didn't want to be in that class. None of my friends are in it and I don't like the teacher."

"Well, we didn't know that," his mother said.

"You didn't know because you don't let me have any say, and then I get angry at you guys."

The therapist quickly interrupted. "Michael, by owning your anger and stating it in a way that accepts responsibility for that anger rather than blaming your parents for it, you've moved the

three of you into a solution-seeking mode. Now you can fix the problem together."

The rest of the family therapy session focused on doing just that. Together, with equal input from everyone, Michael and his parents brainstormed possible solutions to the problem. They chose a plan and talked about ways to implement it. Yes, anger was still present in the room, but fixing blame for that anger was not. By owning his anger, Michael *felt* more in control and, as a result, *acted* more in control.

*****

Darcy had been talking to her best friend, Olivia, on the phone. At the end of their conversation, Darcy approached her father. "Olivia wants to know if I can stay overnight," she told him.

"We call that manner of speaking disowning responsibility for your question," her dad responded. "When I hear a question asked that way, the answer is always no. What we do in this family is take responsibility for our questions by using an 'I' statement. It sounds like this. 'I would like to know if I can stay overnight with Olivia.' When I hear it asked that way, I think it over. Sometimes I say yes and sometimes the answer is no."

Darcy got the message and immediately rephrased her question. "Dad, *I* would like to know if I can stay overnight at Olivia's."

"Tell me more about your plan," her father responded. "I'd like to hear some of the details." The discussion then continued until Olivia and her father reached agreement on the specifics.

*****

Rachael's parents had been divorced for eight months when she started refusing to plan weekend overnight stays with her father.

According to the court ruling, she was to spend every other weekend and one evening during the week at her father's house.

No one knew why Rachael didn't want to go to her father's house. When she was asked about it, all she would say is, "I don't want to go."

Several weeks passed with no change in the situation. Then one evening Rachael's mother, Margaret, overheard a telephone conversation between Rachael and her best friend. "My dad always says that we're going to do something special when I stay at his house and we never do," Rachael complained. "He says that he'll take me to the movies and then we sit and watch TV the whole time I'm there. When I ask him about it, he says we'll do something next time, but we don't. There's no use in planning anything with him. He won't do it anyway."

Margaret knew exactly what was happening. Rachael no longer trusted her father's words. She saw that his words held little meaning. Margaret could understand why Rachael didn't want to make plans with her father and had little interest in going to visit him. She also knew that if the situation was not addressed Rachael could end up resenting her father and feeling confused about her worth as his daughter.

With much apprehension, Margaret passed the information on to her ex-husband and told him that she expected him to either stop promising to do things or to follow through with his promises. Reluctantly, she threatened to get the court involved if he didn't make changes at the next visit.

To Margaret's surprise, Rachael returned from her next weekend visit at her father's with a glowing report. She talked about all the things they had done together, none of them involving sitting in front of the television set.

*****

"I really lucked out today," Ian Phillips informed his mother when he returned home from an afternoon at the library.

"What do you mean?" his mother asked.

"I found just the sources I need to finish my term paper."

"That's exciting. I'm happy for you," his mother responded, "but I'd like you to change your initial statement. It sounded like you were using the language of luck."

"What do you mean?" Ian asked.

"It sounded to me like you gave luck the credit for finding the sources. I'll bet you had more to do with it than luck did," his mother said.

"Well, I did invest two hours of time in the library," Ian admitted. "I spent most of that time looking in the card catalog and tracking down books."

"Just as I suspected," Mrs. Phillips said, smiling at her son. "You didn't really luck out. You simply put forth a strong effort."

"Yeah, I guess I did," Ian said, returning her smile.

*****

Every morning Roger found himself repeatedly reminding his son, Max, "Hurry up and get dressed. You're going to be late for school." Max's predictable response was, "You're making me have to rush." Around and around Roger and Max would go. "You're going to be late." "You're making me hurry."

This happened morning after morning until Roger attended a Parent Talk workshop sponsored by Max's school. That evening in the workshop, Roger learned about choices and the words to use to place responsibility back on his son's shoulders. Armed with new verbal skills, Roger vowed to make the next morning different.

The next day Roger walked confidently into his son's room. As usual, he found Max lying on the floor in his pajamas. Roger looked at the youngster and said calmly, "If you choose to go slow in putting

your clothes on, it's OK. Just know that you'll be choosing either to go to school in your pajamas or to have to rush at the last minute to get dressed in time. You decide." Then he walked out of the room.

Roger took this same approach every morning. Some mornings Max was dressed and ready to go long before it was time to leave. Other mornings he rushed to get dressed and was putting clothes on as he headed out the door to catch the bus. To Roger's surprise, he never went to school in his pajamas.

Roger stopped arguing with his son and taking the blame for his youngster's feeling hurried. He used self-responsible language to let go of the problem and give the responsibility back to Max.

*****

"I can't mow the grass," Roberto told his father. "It's too hot."

"Nothing is too anything," his father responded matter-of-factly.

"Huh?" Roberto replied.

"Nothing is too anything," his father repeated. "'Too' is a word that people use to prevent taking action and following through. 'It's too wet to go outside.' They use it to prevent seeing themselves as able to do something. 'I'm too old or too young to do that.' They use it to avoid taking responsibility. 'I was too mad to think straight.' Some use it to prevent risk or change. 'She's too attractive for me to ask out.' How are you using it?" his father asked.

"Dad, it's 95 degrees. It's too hot to mow the grass," Roberto insisted.

"Nothing is too anything," his father said once again. "It's possible to mow the grass in 95 degree heat. Stop frequently. Drink lots of water. Take long breaks."

"OK, it is possible," Roberto conceded, "but I don't want to do it right now."

"Then you choose not to?" his father asked.

"That's right," said Roberto. "I choose not to right now."

"Thanks for hanging in there with me on this, Roberto," his father said. "Saying that you choose not to mow right now sounds a lot more self-responsible that saying it's too hot. I appreciate you using language that makes your choice conscious."

"Oh, Dad!" Roberto responded with a grin, revealing both his admiration for his father and his frustration with the situation.

*****

Carl watched his son Marcos step out of the car in full soccer gear and place his soccer ball next to the back steps as he took off his shoes before entering the house. The routine was to place all your soccer gear in the sports bag and have it ready for the next practice. Marcos followed the routine in usual fashion, except for the soccer ball, which was left next to the steps.

Two days later, when Marcos was getting ready for soccer practice, the ball was not in his bag. Furious, he turned to his younger brother and began accusing him of taking his ball without permission and not putting it back.

Carl, remembering where the ball had been placed, stepped in to help his younger son, who had no clue why he was being verbally attacked by his brother. "It's not OK to talk to your brother like that," Carl said to Marcos. You're responsible for your own soccer equipment. Your brother had nothing to do with your ball."

"He must have," Marcos shouted.

"No, that's not true," Carl told him. "Take responsibility for your own actions by retracing your steps the other night when you came home from practice and I think you'll figure out what happened to your soccer ball."

With much grumbling, Marcos grabbed his soccer bag and headed out the door. A few minutes later, he returned with his head hanging down and a soccer ball in his hands.

Carl looked at Marcos and said, "I think you need to say something to your brother before we leave."

Marcos walked over to his younger brother and quietly said, "I was wrong in accusing you of doing something with my ball. Next time I'll be more gentle with my words and maybe I'll ask you for some help."

Carl put his arm around Marcos and gave him a hug. "Let's go to soccer practice, boys," he said, and off they went.

The Self-Responsible Language Challenge

Are you ready to make a commitment to speak in self-responsible language? Have you already done so? The items below can help determine your degree of satisfaction with your efforts. Use them to challenge yourself. Set goals for improvement. Celebrate your successes. Move increasingly toward parenting with purpose using the sixth commitment.

Awareness

Do you pay close attention to the language you use when talking to your children? Are you a "Do as I say, not as I do" person when it comes to the language you use? Do you listen to yourself and hear the message you're sending? Are you aware that your children are listening even when you are not talking directly to them?

Integrity

Are you trustworthy? Are you honest and open with the words you use? Do you tell your children what you are planning so they know your intentions? Do your actions reflect those intentions? Or do you say one thing and then do another? Do you tell people what they want to hear? Do you talk about others behind their back? Do

you like to gossip? Your children are listening to your words and watching your behavior to see if they match. Are you doing the same with yourself?

Ownership

Do your children make you mad? Do rainy days get you down? Does sunshine on your shoulder make you happy? Does getting flowers make you smile? Is your work stressing you out? Do sad movies make you cry? Does the evening news disgust you? Do the lyrics of today's songs make you sick? Do tornados or heights scare you? Do your children embarrass you? Do dirty dishes in the sink bother you? Does being around horses (or snakes or sharks) make you nervous? Is work depressing? What message are you sending about owning your feelings?

Teaching

Do you point out to your children that advertisers have a vested interest in having us believe that our happiness, health, and excitement come from their products? Do you show them billboards along the side of the highway that fuel this myth? Do you discuss the commercials on TV and radio and point out to your child what advertisers are really trying to sell? Do you help your child hear the "makes me" language their friends use? Do you encourage your children to confront you when you use "makes me" or "I can't" language?

Impeccability

Are you impeccable with your language? Do you see words as tools? Do you see them as seeds that later take root, sprout, and grow? Do you treat your language patterns as programming that is

influencing your own and your child's biocomputer (mind)? Do you deliberately choose specific words and purposefully construct language patterns that reflect and promote self-responsibility?

Conclusion

Actions speak louder than words, you may be thinking. Or, Be a doer, not a talker. Or, as one workshop participant recently told us, "Words are cheap."

Words are not cheap. They are the most valuable currency you possess if creating self-responsible young people is one of your parenting goals. The words your children use create their thoughts. Their repetitious thoughts become their beliefs. And their beliefs influence their actions. If you want children who demonstrate self-responsible behaviors, begin by teaching them self-responsible language.

The Seventh Commitment

I commit to helping my children develop their inner authority.

I recognize that an inner authority is the only authority my children will take with them everywhere they go. To that end, I strive to make myself dispensable and to assist them in becoming increasingly in charge of themselves and their own lives. I help my children develop their inner authority.

We teach our children to search for solutions and solve many of their own problems. We do this because we know we cannot be with them every minute of their lives. We realize we cannot follow them around forever and take care of their every concern. So we opt for the next best thing: we help them become self-sufficient. We help them learn to take care of themselves. This growth occurs steadily over time as children demonstrate they can handle more of their own affairs and problems and continues until the child is ready to leave home.

Whether our children get married, go off to college, sign up for the armed services, or join the work force, our goal is the same. Our job is to get them ready to function on their own in self-responsible, healthy, productive ways.

As we teach our children to solve their problems and handle life situations, we often direct them to look outside of themselves for answers. We teach them to examine an encyclopedia, read the newspaper, access the Internet, consult experts, and use the library. We teach them to look for a variety of resources for answers, but

rarely do we teach them to look inside themselves.

Each of us has a place inside that knows what is right for us. Whether we call it intuition, conscience, gut-level feeling, listening to God, inner knowing, or trusting your gut, this place is a valuable and often neglected resource for our children. Learning how to access, pay attention to, and respond to that inner authority are important skills. It is our job to make sure our children learn those skills.

Some parents want their children to respond only to an outside authority, that being the parents. That preference is functional and reasonable when a health or safety issue is involved. If a young child is poised to run across the road, we want her to respond to our authority now! But when safety issues are not an issue, teaching the child to respond to an outside authority is often counterproductive.

Children who learn to listen to an outside voice do not learn to trust themselves. They do not develop a strong internal standard or learn to trust their own judgment regarding sex, drugs, alcohol, and other important issues. They become more susceptible to peer pressure than do children who have developed a strong inner authority.

The biggest problem for children trained to listen only to an outside voice occurs in adolescence. At that time in a child's life, the outside voice changes. It shifts from the parent to the peer group. It requires a powerful sense of self to stand in one's peer group at age fourteen and say, "I think I'm going to pass on this. It doesn't fit with what I think is right for me. It violates one of my major values." This is a difficult stance for a child to take with friends. It is doubly tough for a child who has had little practice listening inwardly.

An inner authority is the only authority you take with you everywhere you go. Your teen is not going to call you on her cell phone and say, "Dad, my boyfriend wants me to jump in the back seat of his car with him. What do you think I should do?" That's not going to happen. Your child will make a decision on the spot, based

on her internalized values and conscience. That is, if she is tuned in and listening to that inside voice.

Trusting inner authority is not like a light bulb that parents can turn on when their child becomes thirteen. It doesn't work that way. An inner authority brightens slowly over time and grows brighter with regular use. If the inner voice is discouraged or lies dormant, it dims and grows weaker, depriving children of an important source of knowledge.

Yes, children make mistakes when using their inner authority. As one father reported at a recent workshop, "My seven-year-old son met me at the door last night and informed me, 'I trusted my gut. And my gut said to eat the whole cake, so I did.'" Children make mistakes with spelling. They make mistakes with fractions. And they make mistakes with following their inner authority. That's where debriefing comes in.

Investing time in debriefing your children's successful and unsuccessful attempts to follow their gut-level feeling or listen to God is time well spent. It is a time you can listen to your children, explore their thought processes, and understand their reasoning. It is also a time to communicate your values, concerns, and appreciations. Goal setting can occur during debriefing as you challenge your child to determine what he or she would like to do next time.

Children need adults to clarify and interpret the world around them so they can begin to make sense of what they are feeling and the external world they are experiencing. They need guidance in putting a value system to work and incorporating those values into their being. To help your children do this, it's important to share your personal views, the opinions of the society in which you live, and the religious principles under which your family functions. As they internalize these values, they slowly begin to make decisions based on their own internalized feelings.

Without helping children personalize and make sense out of

values through debriefing and direct teaching, we leave them to make emotional and cognitive sense of the world on their own. This is a difficult task for many children. Often, they don't know what feelings they're experiencing or what to do with them. In an attempt to manage their thoughts and feelings, they act them out, many times in ways that adults interpret as "bad behavior." Without parental guidance in how to respond to their world, children will guide themselves by repeating the same behavior choice or randomly making a different choice, with little or no connection to internal feelings and processes.

By asking your children, "What do you think was going on inside you when you made that decision?" you bring their attention to their inner authority. Children often say, "I don't know," in response to this question. And that's the point. Children don't always know or aren't always aware of what they know. By putting the seventh commitment to work in your family, you're helping your children learn to "know what they know," to listen to themselves and choose behavior based on a clear understanding of the voice within. You are assisting them in connecting with their internal authority.

Please remember that the seventh commitment is about helping your children develop *their own* inner authority. It is not about having them adopt *your* inner authority. The goal is not to have your children do it your way or to think solely the way you think. The goal is to help them learn to think for themselves, to respond out of their own desires, to make choices based on their own internal thoughts and feelings.

Life Examples

Joanna arrived early to pick up her son Timothy from school. As she waited outside his first-grade classroom, she quietly observed the end-of-the-day routine. The children stood in a line waiting to be dismissed. As they waited, the teacher gave each child a sticker

that they placed on the back of their hands. It appeared to Joanna that all the children except for her son received a sticker.

As soon as they arrived home, Joanna inquired about what she had seen. "Timothy," she said, "I noticed the teacher was handing out stickers today. Tell me about that."

"She hands out stickers every day," Timothy stated matter-of-factly.

Curious, Joanna pressed on. "Why does she give stickers?"

"She gives them to the kids that have been good all day," Timothy told her.

"Does she give everyone a sticker?" Joanna asked.

"No," Timothy responded. "Some kids don't get them if they talk too much or don't get their work done."

"I've never seen you with a sticker," Joanna said.

"I don't take them," Timothy told his mother. "I know when I've been good. I don't need a sticker to tell me that."

Joanna smiled and patted Timothy on the head. "I'm happy to hear that," she said as he made his way to the refrigerator.

That day, Joanna confirmed what she had already suspected. Timothy, at age seven, was beginning to develop his inner authority. He was building his own internal picture of good and bad, right and wrong. He didn't need a sticker or candy to motivate him to behave. His motivation came out of his own personal inner desire.

Timothy also didn't need someone else telling him he did a good job. He knew when he did a good job and when he didn't. He knew it on the inside, and he knew what he did to produce his internal feeling.

*****

Brandon Haslette was given three tickets to a Michigan State football game. Since his wife had no interest in football, he invited his thirteen-year-old son, Matt, to accompany him and asked Matt to invite one

of his friends. Matt had three close friends, all responsible youngsters whom Brandon would be happy to include in their Saturday football adventure.

Three days later, Matt approached his dad and announced, "I have a problem. I don't know who to invite to the football game. I have three good friends and I can't make up my mind."

Brandon had an adult solution to the problem. He wanted to suggest that Matt ask Steve. Steve had invited Matt to two Detroit Red Wing games previously, and Brandon wanted Matt to learn a lesson about returning favors, giving back, and remembering those who have helped you in the past. But he didn't suggest Steve. Instead, Brandon bit his tongue and said, "Why don't you check it out inside?"

Matt knew what "Check it out inside" meant. His parents had used that phrase with him many times before. It meant go to your room, turn off anything that makes noise, sit quietly, and see if you can get in touch with an inside feeling. It was his job to check in and listen for his own right answer.

While Matt checked it out inside, Brandon reminded himself that his son didn't need to learn the lesson of payback in this moment. He knew that parenting provides many opportunities for parents to teach lessons and that he would get many more opportunities to help Matt learn about remembering past kindnesses. Better, he thought to himself, that I use this opportunity to give Matt an experience with trusting his own judgment.

Fifteen minutes later Matt appeared and announced, "It's all set. I invited Charlie and he accepted." Matt hadn't picked Steve. As they talked about Matt's selection, Brandon found out that Charlie rarely got to do anything special and Matt's other two friends had parents who arranged frequent interesting adventures for their children. Matt felt it was time for Charlie to have a turn at doing something exciting.

"How did you realize that Charlie needed to do something

exciting?" Brandon asked his son. "It just came to me," Matt said, "as I sat there in my room. It was a feeling I got, and you always tell me I can trust that. So I did."

Brandon smiled and remembered how he had almost suggested Steve an hour earlier. He gave Matt a pat on the back as they parted and then gave another to himself for being alert and wise enough to suggest that Matt check it out inside.

*****

Recently assigned to sub in a third-grade classroom, Christian Miller was moving uneventfully through the day. Thankfully, no behavior problems required his attention. He had followed the detailed lesson plans for math and language arts. Spelling was next on the agenda.

The directions for spelling were simple enough. Christian was instructed to announce a ten-minute study time and then give the students a trial test on their weekly list of words. Students who spelled all words correctly on the trial test would be excused from the final test on Friday.

At the conclusion of the short study time, Christian asked students to clear off their desks and take out a piece of notebook paper. Immediately, seven students sprang from their chairs and headed toward a bookcase at the back of the room. "Whoa," Christian said to them. "Where are you going?"

"We're going to get the blockers," two students answered simultaneously.

"Blockers? What are blockers?" asked the surprised substitute.

"They're what we use to block our papers so other kids can't see them," answered one of the eight year olds.

"They block the other person's view," added another.

Constructed with three 8 x 10 sheets of cardboard taped in the middle, blockers stand upright. They are designed to shield one student's paper from another's eyes.

"No, no, no," Christian told the boys. "We don't need blockers."

"Yes, we do," responded the third-graders.

"Why?" Christian asked.

"Because we'll look at each other's papers," said one child. "Yeah," agreed several others.

"No," Christian countered. "No one will look today. We don't need the blockers."

"We need them because some kids cheat. They look," warned a well-intentioned girl in the back of the room.

"Let me see a show of hands," Christian said. "How many of you are going to look at another's paper?" No hands were raised.

"See, we don't need blockers today," Christian told the class.

"They say they won't, but they will," a student informed the substitute teacher. Heads nodded in agreement.

Undaunted, Christian asked, "How many of you are just saying that you won't look, but you really will?" Still no hands.

"See?" he said again. "No one in this room is going to look."

"We always use blockers," one student persisted. "Mrs. Tattersall wants us to use them so we don't cheat. They block us from cheating," she explained, hoping to get this substitute teacher to appreciate the necessity of blockers.

"OK, we'll use blockers," Christian announced, appearing to finally cave in to the perceived need to use an external object to protect one child's paper from another's need to look. "We'll use blockers," he continued, "only this time we'll use our inside blockers. Looking or not looking at another's paper is an internal decision that each one of you makes. It's something that happens on the inside of you. If each of you chooses to use your inside blocker, we won't need outside blockers. Things like honesty, integrity, respect, and caring are decisions that each of us makes on the inside. When you make an inside decision, the outside takes care of itself. Outside blockers are only needed when the inside blockers have not been turned on. How about if we play with using our inside blockers today and see how that goes?" Christian

challenged the room full of eight year olds. "Let's see how well your inside blockers are working. Are you willing to turn them on and see what happens?"

"Yes," several students responded, finally conceding to the relentless challenge of their substitute teacher.

"OK. Number your papers from one to fifteen. Put your name in the upper right-hand corner. Turn on your internal blocker. Here we go."

The spelling test proceeded without incident. Students practiced spelling words, and they practiced using their inside blockers.

*****

Tony was on the roof of the house replacing a few shingles that had blown loose in a recent storm when he heard Carl, his five-year-old son, yell from below, "Dad, can I climb up the ladder?" Tony quickly set down his tools and headed for the ladder, calling, "Wait right there. I'm coming down."

As Tony started down the ladder, his wife, Karyn, came around the corner of the house and grabbed Carl. "What are you doing, Tony?" she asked.

"I'm coming down to help him climb the ladder," Tony replied.

"He can't go up there. He's too young." Karyn's concern was evident in her face as well as her voice.

"I'm going to help him learn about ladders and climbing. I'll show you what I mean." As soon as Tony's feet hit the ground, he bent down and said to his son, "Carl, ladders are dangerous. It's not safe to climb a ladder without a grownup to help you. Please remember to always have a grownup help you. Let me help you now."

Tony guided Carl to the first rung of the ladder, showed him how to hold onto the sides, and encouraged him to take a step up to the next rung. As soon as Carl was firmly planted on the next rung,

Tony said, "Now, Carl, stop and feel inside. Can you climb down from here?"

"Yes," Carl replied.

"OK, try another step. Only go up as high as you feel comfortable and know you can climb back down by yourself."

Twenty minutes passed as Carl repeatedly climbed up one or two rungs and then back down. He attempted to go to the third rung on several occasions but stopped short of putting both feet firmly on that rung. Each time, Tony encouraged Carl to check on his feelings and only go as high as his comfort allowed. When they finished, Tony again reminded Carl about using a ladder only when an adult helped him. Carl agreed.

Climbing a ladder was not the only lesson Carl learned that day. Through the ladder experience, Tony was helping his young son learn to check it out inside and to trust his feelings. This was a lesson that would extend far beyond that of learning to climb a ladder.

******

"My roommates are heading for trouble," Sarah informed her parents on her first weekend home from college.

"What do you mean?" her father asked.

"They're wild. They stay out all night, drink, and cut classes. One of them has had sex with three different guys that I know of."

"Must have had really permissive parents," Sarah's mother said.

"No. Just the opposite," Sarah responded. "They both come from families where they were highly controlled. It's like they've never had a chance to try anything, so they're doing everything all at once. Now that the person who controlled them isn't around, they don't know how to control themselves. Their accelerators are working, but they don't know how to use their brakes."

"That's too bad," Sarah's father observed.

"Yes, it is," Sarah agreed. "I certainly am grateful you allowed me to make some mistakes growing up. Thanks for encouraging me to trust my own judgment even at those times when I didn't appear too smart."

"You're welcome," both parents said in unison.

*****

Every Saturday morning Mark took his son, Kevin, to the local home improvement store to look at tools and watch the forklift lower stacks of lumber from the top shelf. This was Mark's way of connecting with his toddler and giving his wife a much-needed break from a long week of parenting.

As Mark pulled into a parking space near the front door, Kevin began to whine and kept repeating, "I don't want to. I don't want to."

"What don't you want to?" Mark asked him.

"I don't want to see a forklift," came the whiny response.

"Oh, it will be fun, like always," Mark told his son, pulling him from the car seat and heading for the entrance.

Ten minutes later Mark heard a loud bang, followed by several screams. As he rounded a corner with Kevin in tow, a forklift bumped a stack of lumber on the top shelf, sending the entire bundle to the floor. Lumber flew everywhere, knocking other items off the shelves below in its descent. Mark pulled his son back around the corner and fell to the ground on top of him. To everyone's surprise and relief, no one was hurt.

Mark quickly exited the building cradling his son in his arms. As he strapped him into the seat, Mark looked at Kevin and said, "Next time I'll listen to your intuition and trust that you might know some things that I don't."

*****

As state police officers, both Carl and Maria knew the dangers of

child abduction. They were involved in school educational programs and were on search and rescue teams. Their message extended far beyond that of stranger danger. They taught children how to recognize dangerous moments and identify safe people in case of an emergency.

Carl and Maria put their teaching into practice by taking their own children, ages eight and five, to the mall and grocery store for training sessions. The training consisted of having one of the kids choose a person to go up to and ask what time it was. Later, Carl and Maria sat and talked with their children about how it felt approaching the person they chose and why they didn't ask a different person. They discussed options of other people to talk to and who to approach in case of an emergency

The point of the exercise was to help their children develop a feeling for who was safe and who was not. The children were learning to listen to their instincts and to trust their inner authority.

Carl and Maria saw these teaching moments as an important piece in helping their children be safe. Their hope was that an emergency would never occur in which the children would have to use the skills they were learning, but they wanted them to be ready if it should. The result was that their children were developing an inner authority they could use for the rest of their lives when making everyday decisions.

*****

As his family walked through the front gates of Sea World, Dale handed his seven-year-old son, Michael, the map and said, "Today you can be the one in charge of how we get to where we want to go. I'll help you use this map and you can decide which direction to take."

After each show, the family of five sat together and chose the next show to see. Michael then consulted the map and led the way. When the path split and a decision was needed about which way to

go, Dale helped Michael look over his options and then allowed him to make the final decision. Sometimes they went the long way around. Other times they would pass the same landmarks two or three times before reaching their destination.

At first, the process was frustrating for the family, but soon Michael began to trust his decision-making ability. By midday, he had put the map in his pocket and begun recognizing his surroundings. When he was not sure where to go, he would stop and think. Once he asked a park worker for help. Another time he identified signs that gave directions. On several occasions, he chose a direction based on a hunch, saying, "I think it's this way."

At the end of the evening, Michael was confident in his ability to lead the family out of the park and to their car. That day he learned to handle struggles and overcome adversity. He gained strength in trusting his ability to figure things out for himself.

Developing Inner Authority Challenge

Are you interested in helping your children develop an inner authority? Have you already made the seventh commitment? Use the items below as a self-testing device to assess your current level of implementation and determine your degree of satisfaction with your efforts in each area. Where is there room for improvement? Set goals toward that end. Celebrate your successes. Use the seventh commitment to move ever closer toward parenting with purpose.

Dispensability

Are you indispensable to your children? Do they have trouble functioning without you? Have you intentionally set it up that way? Do you allow your children to take risks and increasingly venture away from you? Do you behave like the mother robin and push them out of the nest on occasion? Do you encourage them to fly on

their own? Do you provide the space for them to do so? If not now, when?

Ultimate Authority

Do you teach obedience no matter what the circumstances? Do you send your children "Stop listening to yourself" messages? Does your behavior communicate, "Listen to me. Listen to us. Follow our rules. We know what is best for you. We have THE way"? If so, you may have forgotten that it is easier to ignore an outside command than one that comes from within.

Support

Do you provide the support necessary for your children to test their wings? Do you encourage them to trust their inner authority? Are you helping them feel secure while they test the waters of real life without you? Can you take pride in that or does it feel scary to you?

Parent Talk

Do you hear yourself saying things like, "Check it out inside," or "Check in"? Do you ask your children to "give it the tummy test"? Do you say, "You decide," and ask later about the decision and the reasons behind it. Do you encourage your children to check themselves rather than expect you to check *on* them?

Debriefing

Do you invest the time to process your children's decisions and choices with them? Do you do more listening or telling? Do you communicate your values in a nonthreatening manner? Do you help them come to their own conclusions about how well they're doing

rather than telling them how well they're doing? Do you help them self-assess and self-evaluate so they can develop a strong internal standard?

Modeling

When was the last time you let your children see you check it out inside? Do you stop when something inside you says, "This isn't right"? Are you willing to say, "I don't want to do this. It just doesn't feel right to me"? Do you say to your children, "I need to take a moment and see what this feels like inside"? Do you make decisions without ever letting your children know how you got to the decision, or do you share your internal process with them as you go through it? Do you meditate or pray about a decision? Do you sit down together as a family and process each person's feelings about a decision? Do you model how to use and develop an inner authority?

Rescuing

It's difficult for many parents to let their children struggle with a decision so they move in quickly with the answer, thinking they're being helpful. They rescue their children, denying them opportunities to check it out inside. They provide answers where exploration is needed. They take charge of the child when the child needs to take charge of himself. Where are you in respect to rescuing? Are you quick to move in and show your children the way? Do you tell them how they should feel, or do you help them understand the feelings they are having?

Identifying Feelings

Do you help your child understand feelings? Do you provide guidance in identifying feelings of safety and security? Do you help your

children recognize how it feels to be angry versus how it feels to be hurt? When your child is having an emotional moment, do you process the emotions with him, or do you tell him to stop being so emotional?

Conclusion

Applying your own yardstick, developing your own ethics, creating an internal standard, creating a personal vision of truth, trusting your inner authority are not always valued by adults in positions of authority. In fact, thinking for oneself often leads to disapproval in our society.

The main question becomes, What do we really want for our children? Questions that help us answer that question include: Do we want our children to be blindly obedient or to think for themselves? Do we want them to mind or to think through their choices and the potential consequences of a situation and decide for themselves? Do we want them to follow our personal truths or to create their own? Do we want them to follow a set of rules laid down by others or create a personal code of ethics for themselves?

If you're not sure how to answer these questions, why not check it out inside? Your answers are in there somewhere. Why not listen and respond?

The Eighth Commitment

I commit to modeling the message.

I recognize that attitudes are more easily caught than taught. I know that children pay more attention to what I do than to what I say. I will walk my talk. I will BE the message I want to deliver to my children. I model the message.

What if your life IS the message? What if how you choose to live your life is the central learning that your children have come to earth to discover? What if the lessons you design, the tips you impart, the learning experiences you arrange, the lectures you deliver, the advice you share, the words of wisdom you speak to your children do not have as much impact on them as the way you live?

Young children need only observe a behavior a few times to be able to reproduce it. They repeat the words they hear. They imitate the actions they see. Adolescents, too, learn by watching and imitating. The mental model we create in their minds and hearts by our behavior is a powerful teaching for children of all ages.

The potential for modeling exists in every moment. You can never turn it off. Telling your children "I'm not going to model for the next hour, so don't pay attention to what I do" does not work. Your children are still watching. They are taking it all in. And they are being influenced by your behaviors. Do you remember the familiar adage, "Actions speak louder than words"? It's true.

When your child behaves in a manner that you feel is inappropriate, look at yourself first. Check your attitude. Notice

what you are doing. Listen to your tone of voice. Ask yourself, What role am I playing in my child acting this way? What am I modeling here?

As you implement a parenting strategy, stop and check yourself. Consider what you could change in your own behavior that would encourage your child to change his or her behavior. *Be the change you wish to see in your children.* Change yourself first and notice how often your child responds appropriately.

Life Examples

"If it's my boss, tell him I'm not home," Latisha told her husband within earshot of their two children. Her kids were quietly completing homework at the kitchen table. They heard.

Ironically, this is the same mom who disciplined her eight-year-old son earlier in the day for lying about the chocolate chip cookies that mysteriously disappeared while she was grocery shopping.

✝✝✝✝✝

Allan stopped at a roadside vegetable stand to buy fresh corn and tomatoes. His three children piled out of the car to get in on the action of picking out the preferred produce. With the selection process complete, Allan paid his six-dollar tab with what he thought was a five-dollar bill plus a one. As he turned to leave, the farmer said, "You gave me too much money. You gave me a one and a twenty." The man's honesty was not lost on David's three children, nor was it lost on the farmer's own teenage son who stood nearby helping another customer.

*****

"I don't know why my child takes things out of other kids' desks," Mr. Fuller told the elementary school principal. "He knows better than to steal. The real surprise to me is that he was taking markers. We have a ton of markers where I work. All he has to do is tell me he needs some and I bring them home from work for him." Surprisingly, it never occurred to Mr. Fuller that he was modeling the exact behavior he wished to discourage in his child.

*****

Bob was fishing with his teenage son, Tom, in the early evening. As the sun was setting and twilight spread over the lake, the fish began biting regularly. Before they realized it, darkness had settled in and it was time for the father/son duo to head to shore.

Bob was reeling in the last line when he heard an unfamiliar voice. In the fishing frenzy, Bob had forgotten to turn on the boat lights, and a DNR officer had pulled alongside their boat to discuss the matter. After briefly talking over the issue, the officer handed Bob a $100 fine that covered several minor boating infractions that he had observed.

On shore, while packing up the fishing gear, Tom found a large, expensive flashlight. "Look," he told his dad excitedly, "the DNR guy left us a little gift. I guess that's what he gets for writing us that ticket." Bob didn't say a word.

When the truck was packed, Bob and Tom jumped in the front seat, but instead of taking the route home, Bob surprised his son by heading to the other side of the lake and the local DNR office, a destination 20 miles out of their way.

When they arrived at the DNR office, Bob went inside and asked to speak to the officer whose name was on the bottom of the ticket. Tom figured his dad was going to give him an earful. When the officer appeared, he too figured he was in for an earful. Instead, Tom and the officer both learned a valuable lesson.

"Did you lose a flashlight this evening?" Bob asked the officer.

"Yes," the man replied, looking somewhat stunned.

"I have it. I'll be right back," Bob told him. A moment later, he returned with the flashlight in hand and gave it to the officer. Still stunned, all the officer could do was offer a simple, "Thank you."

On the drive home, Tom inquired about his dad's behavior. "How come you returned the flashlight after how that guy treated you?" Bob smiled and said, "My son, the man was simply doing his job, and it wasn't my flashlight to keep."

*****

Can you imagine parents giving their children formal gossip lessons? Can you envision them teaching their children the specific skills necessary to become proficient at the art of gossiping? That is exactly what David and Samantha Welder do when they talk about other people in front of their children. Through the evening gossip sessions that include talking about friends, relatives, and other children, David and Samantha are training their own children to duplicate their behaviors, attitude, and style of language.

*****

In a recent phone call, Martha received some distressing news from the administrator that oversees the daycare center her daughter attends. Three-year-old Abigail had been biting some of the other children. This time, she had left teeth marks on another child.

Martha had been informed of the first two incidents earlier in the week. She had been helping Abigail understand that biting is inappropriate since she took the first call on Monday.

In her frustration, Martha explained to the daycare administrator that she had talked with Abigail about her biting and thought she

understood the seriousness of the problem. Martha said, "To let her know how it feels for the other children, I even bit her on the arm. I guess I didn't bite her hard enough."

What Martha didn't realize is that she was teaching Abigail that biting other people is one way to get them to do what you want.

*****

Carlos and Richard had reason to celebrate. Their new book had just been published, and the first copies had arrived from the printers. They made plans to have dinner at an expensive restaurant and celebrate their joint accomplishment. Since toasting their book with a glass of wine was on the agenda, they made plans to hire a designated driver. Richard's two teenagers and Carlos's three preschoolers overheard the telephone conversation that arranged for the designated driver. When the driver arrived, both sets of children sat in the Cadillac witnessing a parent living one of their beliefs—that drinking and driving don't mix.

*****

Michael came in the door from school holding a man's wallet. "Mom, look what I found when I stepped off the bus. It was just lying there," he told his mother. "Wow, there's a ton of money in it, too!"

Taking the wallet from her son, the concerned mother opened it and looked at the driver's license. "This guy is from around here," she said. "Maybe we can find his number in the phone book."

Within minutes, Michael's mom had found the number, given the owner a call, and told him where they lived. He arrived 20 minutes later and, with relief and pleasure, picked up an intact wallet, money and all.

Model the Message Challenge

Where do you stand on the commitment of modeling the message? The questions below will help you challenge yourself to determine how closely your parenting style fits with the eighth commitment. Are there areas of which you're proud? Do you see others you would like to improve? Can you find a growing edge, a strategy you would like to work on right way?

Exercise

Do you model the importance of regular exercise in your life? Are you a runner, a walker, or a racquetball player? Do you participate in an exercise class, take aerobics, or work out in your basement? It matters less what form of exercise you choose and more that it is visible to your children. Obesity in children is rapidly becoming a national crisis. More children are less active than ever before. What kinds of exercise habits are you modeling for *your* children?

Personal Habits

What messages do you model for your youngsters by what you put in your mouth? What kind of food, drink, pills, or tobacco do they see you using? Do you eat nutritiously in appropriate amounts? Or is eating fast food and junk food the behavior your children learn to emulate? Do you use cigarettes, cigars, or chewing tobacco? What liquids do you ingest? Water, soda, beer, hard liquor? Your eating, drinking, and smoking habits are sending a message to your children. Is it the one you want them receiving?

Parenting

Did you know you are teaching your children to parent? One simple fact of parenting is that most people parent their children the same

way in which they themselves were parented. Your behavior is showing your child what it means to be a man or a woman. It is also teaching them lessons about being a daddy or a mommy.

Love

Every child spells love T-I-M-E. Does the amount of time you invest in your children equate with your beliefs about the importance of parenting? Your presence or lack of presence in your children's lives is sending them messages about their importance and about your love. Do you create the time to play catch, shoot baskets, throw water balloons, help with homework, attend the dance recital, play checkers, read bedtime stories, or coach the soccer team? Do you spell love the same way your child does: T-I-M-E?

Crisis

How do you suppose children learn to deal with a crisis? They learn by watching adults deal with a crisis. Are you teaching that a crisis leads to blame and punishment or to a search for solutions? Is spilled milk a crisis or an opportunity to teach a lesson about how to handle milk efficiently? When a crisis presents itself in your family, what are you teaching your children by how you choose to handle it?

Communicating Feelings

What type of communication style do you model for your children? When you're angry, do you hold it inside and refuse to talk, giving others "the silent treatment"? Or do you say, "I'm angry. I want to talk about why I'm feeling this way"? Are you prone to yelling and swearing, or to confronting with gentle words? When you're feeling hurt, do you go off alone, stuffing your feelings and refusing to talk

about them? Or do you say, "I need some time alone right now. I'll let you know when I'm ready to talk about how I feel"?

Seeking Help

When you're stuck and not sure what to do next, do you ask for help? Many children do not seek help because they don't know how. They don't see Dad stop and ask for directions when he's lost. They don't hear Mom ask Dad to help fold the laundry. They don't hear a parent say, "I don't know the answer to that. Let's get some help."

Children need to be introduced to the strategies involved in asking for help—knowing who to ask, choosing appropriate words, locating available resources—by parents who model effective help-seeking behaviors.

Do you regularly ask others for help? Do you ask your child for help?

Affection

Do you hold your partner's hand in view of your children? Do you hug or kiss your partner in your child's presence? Do you hug or kiss a close friend in your child's presence? Are you as affectionate with members of the same sex as you are with members of the opposite sex? Do your children see you being affectionate with people of origins different from that of your family? Why not help your child see that people are lovable and that affection is about showing care and concern for other human beings?

Disagreement

Do you argue in front of your children? It is permissible to argue in your children's presence provided you also problem-solve and seek resolution in front of them as well.

Do you model how to "fight fair" while resolving an issue? Do your children hear yelling, name-calling, and foul language? Do they hear you blame and shame? Do they see you destroying property to prove your point? Are you teaching them that it takes increased volume to communicate effectively? Or do they observe you alternately listening attentively and making your case in a respectful tone?

Do your children hear you negotiate, ask for clarification, compromise, or agree to disagree? Do they see you apply a solution and evaluate that solution's effectiveness?

Aggression

Do you yell to stop your child from yelling, or spank your child when she takes a sibling's toy? If so, you are modeling the very behavior that you are attempting to eliminate. When you try to stop your child from being aggressive by overpowering her, by taking a position of authority, or by intimidation, you are using a form of aggression to stop aggression.

Aggression is learned. In one research study, 75 percent of aggressive behavior by children ages 6 to 16 was in response to a parent's suggestion. The children were simply following the directions of parents who told them, "Stand up for yourself," "Hit her back," "Prove you're a man." Are you teaching your children to use aggression to stop aggression?

Separation and Divorce

When it's time to say goodbye, whether the situation involves divorce, moving across the country, or starting a different job, your behavior speaks volumes to your child.

Many people use anger to separate from others because it makes leaving seem easier and less painful. Becoming angry creates

feelings of animosity and resentment, resulting in a gap in the bond with the person being left and the one doing the leaving.

How are you modeling separating? Do your children see you doing it with care and concern? Do you show your children how to leave peacefully? Can you model for them how to move to a new situation or relationship with a kind and gentle heart?

Grieving

Do you let your children see your sadness and your tears when you cry? Whether you know it or not, you're modeling for them how to grieve a loss.

As children develop, many things come and go in their lives. This includes toys, clothes, crib, toddler bed, security blanket, and pets. Perhaps they even lose a grandparent or primary family member. Can you be sad and cry with them? Or do you tell them to "get over it," or that "everything will be all right"?

The way you grieve demonstrates for your children how to grieve. Do you want them to isolate themselves, become depressed, harbor resentment or anger, and avoid responsibilities? Or do you want them to ask for the space they need, express sadness, cherish memories, and remain accessible? The choice is yours, and you communicate that choice through your behavior.

Conclusion

Modeling is a powerful teaching device available to all parents. It is always in use, whether you're aware of it or not. Look at your life and how you choose to live it. Are your actions congruent with your beliefs and spiritual principles? Are your behaviors and attitudes teaching your children what you want them to learn? If not, why not commit to modeling the message?

The Ninth Commitment

I commit to seeing my child as teacher.

I recognize that my children are in my life as much so I can learn from them as they are so they can learn from me. I am open to the lessons my children offer me and honor them for helping me learn and grow. I see my child as teacher.

We tend to think that children are in our lives so they can learn from us. They come into the world knowing little, and it is our job to help them learn much. So we teach them how to walk, ride a bike, and hit a baseball with a bat. We help them acquire language, values, and table manners. We help them learn to dress themselves, divide fractions, and drive a car. Indeed, a major parenting function is that of teacher.

One way of perceiving the parent/child relationship, then, is that of parent as teacher and child as learner. Another way of seeing this relationship, one that is less often considered, is that of child as teacher and parent as learner.

Could it be that children enter our lives so that we can learn from them as much as they can learn from us? Perhaps they are present in our lives so we can learn to change a diaper, drive safely, or improve our knowledge of nutrition. Maybe they are here so we can develop skills of assertiveness or negotiation or our capacity for forgiveness.

The ninth commitment is a pledge to see your child as teacher. It is a reminder that your children have much to offer in helping you

learn and grow as a parent and as a human being. Perhaps your child is offering you lessons in the importance of play, spontaneity, or getting up after you fall down. The parenting or personal growth area your child is helping you with could be about unconditional love, anger management, or acceptance of differences. Their gift could be teaching you about patience, trusting your own judgment, or learning tolerance.

To observe the ninth commitment you must first be aware that your child is offering you a lesson. Then you must be willing to focus on *your* lesson rather than on your child's lesson. In parenting with purpose, the question, What is it that I need to *know*?, becomes more important than asking, What is it that I need to *do*? You observe your own internal reaction to a situation and explore what that internal reaction is telling you. You become aware of your feelings and how those feelings are influencing your response to your child. You look for *your* lesson. You become the student and you allow your child to be the teacher.

To open yourself to the lessons that your child is offering you, observe his or her behavior. When you notice a particular behavior that calls for you to step in as the adult with structure or nurture, ask yourself, What can *I* learn here? Before applying a discipline strategy to correct your *child's* behavior, look at your own behavior. Consider learning *your* lesson first. Once you have learned *your* lesson, you may be surprised to find that your child may no longer need to manifest the "problem" behavior as a learning device for *you*.

Ask yourself questions that lead you to your learning opportunity: What can I learn from this? Am I in some unconscious way modeling the inappropriate behavior that I'm observing in my child? What could *I* change that would help him modify this behavior? What is she trying to tell me by behaving this way? What is it that I need to know that I don't currently know?

Your children could be calling you to learn patience when they

repeatedly make the same mistakes. Your daughter could be encouraging you to refine your anger management skills when she yells, "I hate you. This isn't fair." Your teenage son might be calling you to learn more about tolerance and accepting differences when he announces to the family that he is gay. There are lessons you need to learn as a parent, and your child is present to help you learn them.

A useful belief to cultivate in connection with the ninth commitment is: *When the parent is ready, the child appears.* Assume the attitude that if a challenging child enters your life, it is no accident or random quirk of fate. He or she is there for a reason. Either you already have the skills to interact with and guide this child or you are ready to acquire them.

Do you have a special needs child? He may be present in your life to help you learn about dyslexia, hyperactivity, or autism. Maybe patience, understanding, or commitment is the lesson you are being called to learn. Whatever the challenge, you must be ready or this child would not be presenting himself to you at this moment. Remember, when the parent is ready, the child appears.

Another benefit of being willing to see your children as teacher is the realization that not only can they teach *you* and help you learn and grow, they can teach *themselves*. You don't have to be the one to teach them everything they need to know. Parents, instructors, therapists, and facilitators all play a part in a child's learning. But to commit to seeing the child as teacher is to go one step further and recognize that children can and do teach themselves.

Children intuitively know what they need to learn. They naturally involve themselves in activities and choose behaviors that help them learn and grow. They learn continuously as an innate part of living. The choices they make and the behaviors they exhibit are integral parts of their learning process.

Children choose the learning process that is best for them at any given moment. At times, they may need your direction and

guidance. At other times, they may need you to back off and allow the learning to come from someone or something else. They know what they need, and the ninth commitment asks you to trust that knowing.

Your child's learning process could be facilitated by you, by another parent, by a different adult in your child's life, by a sibling, a peer, an experience, a consequence, a struggle, or a mistake. Unless the situation involves a health or safety issue, in making the ninth commitment you are asked to allow the child to decide the path from which his or her learning will come. You are called upon to be the observer and the learner while allowing your child to be the teacher.

Life Examples

Before he went to Afghanistan, Stan Jenkins was trained to give and follow orders. He was taught to kill and use violence on others before violence was used on him. During his tour of duty, he honed his skills with daily practice.

When he returned home to his wife and two young children, Stan was, in his own words, an authoritarian bully. He believed his wife and children belonged to him. Getting his children to obey was the way he thought a father was supposed to be.

One day, as he stood yelling in front of his four-year-old son, he noticed the pain and terror in his child's eyes. That pain scared him, and he entered counseling the following week. Slowly, Stan began to change his parenting style. For several months, he let his wife take the lead in disciplining and studied her behaviors and the children's reactions. He learned from both his wife and his children.

When Stan began to use new parenting skills with his family, he requested their assistance. He asked that they resist any harsh or unfair treatment. He told them, "If you catch me acting like a bully or a dictator, please call me on it immediately." Because he was

much bigger, stronger, and louder than his children were, Stan arranged for a hand signal from his family to serve as a warning that he was getting out of control. The peace sign became the agreed upon signal.

Although the signal had been set and permission to use it given, the children were suspicious. They were unsure if it would work or if it might backfire and cause their dad to become even more angry.

Stan reported that one day, as he was giving his six-year-old son a severe tongue-lashing, the boy ducked his head under his outstretched arm and gave the signal. "It stopped me like a lightning bolt," Stan said. "In mid-sentence I started grinning, then broke into laughter. I grabbed my son in my arms and kissed his frightened face until we were both laughing and crying. I held him for a long time and thanked him repeatedly. I don't recall why I was so angry," Stan continued, "but it doesn't matter anymore. Thanks to my son's courage, it was the last time I used physical or emotional violence against my children or anyone else."

*****

Enrique and his three-year-old son, Ramón, visited the downtown farmers' market together for the first time. They stopped at every booth to look at all the fresh fruits and vegetables grown by the local farmers. As they stood hand in hand in front of the first vendor's booth, Ramón pulled and tugged at his father's arm and whined. Enrique pulled back and told his son to stop behaving that way while he was attempting to shop.

This whine-and-pull routine was repeated at several stands. When the two stopped in front of an apple display, Ramón reached up and grabbed an apple from the bottom row, sending the neatly stacked pile to the ground. Exasperated, Enrique yelled at his son, "Why did you do that? Now we have to pick them all up!"

As he bent down and began helping Ramón replace the apples

on the shelf, Enrique made an interesting discovery. He noticed that from his knees he could see nothing but the bottom of the shelf and a sea of legs on the other side of the booth.

A feeling of remorse rushed through Enrique's body when he realized that at Ramón's eye level he could see very little and was being excluded from the shopping experience. Pulling the apples from the shelf was a way for Ramón to help his father see the farmers' market from the viewpoint of a three year old.

Enrique quickly replaced the remaining fallen apples on the shelf with no additional chastisement or words of disapproval for his son. When the last apple had been returned to the shelf, he looked at Ramón and said, "Thank you for helping me see through your eyes." Then he hoisted his son onto his shoulders and the two continued their shopping adventure, each from a new perspective.

*****

Richard Coddington's mother had recently died after a two-year battle with cancer. The disease had slowly but steadily worn her down and Richard as well. He was working full time and frequently drove the two hundred miles to his mother's bedside to offer support and encouragement. At the end, in the midst of his own grief, Richard handled the details of the funeral and consoled his elderly father.

When the service and burial were over and friends and relatives had paid their final respects, Richard sat down at the kitchen table to rest. His four-year-old son, Peter, immediately approached him and said, "Daddy, let's play." Richard declined the invitation, explaining that he was tired and sad because Gramma had died. "I know that, Daddy," Peter persisted. "That's why you play, so you won't feel sad. So you'll feel better."

So they played. Richard and Peter went to a nearby pond and threw stones in the water. They made frogs jump. They got their feet and pants legs wet. They smelled the flowers growing along

the bank. When they came back to the house, Richard discovered that Peter was right. They both felt better.

*****

Jean Claude was replacing a broken fence board when he dropped the box of nails into the grass. "Darn it! How am I going to find all those?" he exclaimed in exasperation. His four-year-old son, Stephen, who had been watching his father closely, quickly chimed in, "I know."

"You know what?"

"I know how you can find all the nails."

Interested in hearing what solution his four year old would come up with, Jean Claude pressed him. "How do you suggest I find all these nails?"

"Well, *you* pick up all the ones you can see, and *I'll* go in the house and get a magnet off the refrigerator. We can let the magnet get the rest for us."

A grin came across Jean Claude's face as he thought, I might have been down on my hands and knees for a long time before I came up with that idea. Still smiling, he looked at Stephen and said, "That's a great idea. I'll get started on picking these up. You . . ."

Before he could finish, Stephen had disappeared around the corner of the fence toward the house, running as fast as his little legs could take him. Moments later, he returned with a refrigerator magnet in hand and a grin to match that of his father.

*****

"Come out, Mom! You have to see this!" were the words eleven-year-old Juanita used to entice Rosita out of her kitchen and into the back yard. There, at the other end of the field, was the most magnificent rainbow Rosita had ever seen.

Amidst her mother's "ohhhs" and "ahhhs," Juanita ran to get her camera. As she began snapping off pictures, Rosita warned, "You're wasting film. The scene is way too expansive to capture with that camera." Her daughter kept on clicking.

A year later, leafing through a photo album, Rosita came across a dazzling picture of a rainbow. Her daughter had captured the entire scene by shooting four pictures and pasting them together. She had placed it in the album without telling her mother.

Rosita learned some valuable lessons that day. She learned that expansive landscapes can indeed be captured if you use your creativity. She also learned from her daughter's actions the wisdom of keeping the words, "I told you so," to yourself.

*****

Ten-year-old Jerry came flying into the house swearing never to do anything with Chilly again. Whatever had happened was Chilly's fault. Chilly was mean. He was unfair. He was a backstabbing traitor. He was the worst of the worst.

Chilly was Jerry's best friend and lived across the street. But, on this night, Jerry announced that Chilly was never, ever coming into Jerry's house again. He was not welcome. Not for the next hundred years.

The dinner meal that night was a bit quiet. Everybody liked Chilly, so there was a certain gloom in the air. Then the doorbell rang.

Jerry ran to get it and returned with Chilly by his side. "Mom, can Chilly have some cake with us?" he asked.

"Of course he can," his mother responded. "But what about those comments you just shared about Chilly?"

Jerry thought about that for a moment, then said, "One thing you have to know about me and Chilly, Mom. We're good at forgetting."

*****

Jimmy Nelson had saved his lawn mowing money for several months to purchase a dirt bike he saw in the newspaper. He talked it over with his parents and they agreed that he could buy the motorcycle, but he would be solely responsible for its upkeep, gas, accessories, and anything else that owning it involved.

After two weeks of riding around the family farm with his friends, Jimmy found himself spending more time trying to keep the dirt bike running than he did riding it. He spent hour after hour almost every day repairing some malfunction. On occasion, days went by without his being able to ride it at all.

With each passing day, Jimmy's frustration and anger grew. It often escalated into screaming, slamming doors, and throwing tools. Every day Mrs. Nelson listened to her son rant and rave and throw tantrums without saying a word. Finally, feeling something needed to be done, she told her husband that the motorcycle had to go.

Mr. Nelson agreed that something needed to be done, but he didn't feel that getting rid of the motorcycle was the best remedy. Instead, he created a space in the barn just for Jimmy's tools and the motorcycle. His parents informed him that anything related to fixing the motorcycle needed to remain in the barn. That included tantrums as well as tools.

It was difficult at times for Jimmy's mother to not step in and take over. She desperately wanted to help her son with his anger. Yet she was able to confine her interventions and redirection to only those times when his anger spilled outside the barn. She reminded herself frequently that it was not her job to teach this lesson in anger management.

In time, Jimmy's anger diminished. He spent less time in the barn and found other interests with his friends. At the end of the summer, he asked his dad for help in getting the motorcycle running

so he could sell it. For several nights they worked together to get the dirt bike back in working condition. Jimmy took one last spin around the farm and set the bike out front with a "for sale" sign on it. On the way back to the house, he said, "Dad, thanks for letting me figure this one out on my own."

Putting his arm around his son, Mr. Nelson replied, "Your mom might appreciate hearing those words, too, son."

*****

"Daddy, Daddy, come look at my picture," six-year-old Jaynie Carlsen begged her father.

"Not now, honey," Mr. Carlsen replied. "I'm busy. I'll look at it later."

"Please, Daddy. It's a picture of our whole family."

"Jaynie, I can't do it right now," her father told her. "I have to finish this project."

"But Daddy, I want you to see my picture of our family."

"Hang it up on the refrigerator for me. I'll look at it later."

Later, when he had finished his project, Jaynie's father called her in from outside and asked her to show him the picture.

"See, there's me," Jaynie informed him, pointing to a lovely stick figure portrait, "and there's Mollie. See, we're each holding Mom's hand." The family dog was lying on the floor, asleep.

"What a lovely picture," Mr. Carlsen told his proud daughter. "Thank you for sharing it with me. I'll keep it right here on the refrigerator where I can look at it every day." And with that, he went back to his computer and Jaynie went out to play.

A few moments later, unexplainably uneasy and unable to concentrate, the distracted father went back to look at the picture.

Then he went to the door and called to Jaynie. "Come on in here a minute, will you?" he asked his young daughter. "I want you to show me your picture one more time."

After listening to another rendition of the creation of the family portrait, Mr. Carlsen remarked, "Seems to be someone missing here. How come I'm not in this picture?"

"Oh, you're there. You're just in the computer room working," Jaynie informed him.

Seeing My Child as Teacher Challenge

Where do you stand on the ninth commitment? Are you able to see your child as the teacher? Do you look for *your* lesson in the parenting situation, or do you focus entirely on the lesson you believe your child should learn? The items below will help you examine how you currently see the parent/child relationship. Read them over and think them through. Use them to help you discern whether you have created a balance in seeing yourself as learner as well as teacher.

Expertise

Do you see yourself as the expert in all parent/child interactions? Do you find time to let your child be the expert? Can you slip into the role of learner on occasion and allow your child to take the lead?

Focus

Are you able to look for *your* lesson in each parenting situation? Can you stay focused on what you need to learn, or does your mind keep bringing you back to the lesson you think your child needs to

be learning? Can you simultaneously learn your lesson while teaching your child her lesson? Over which one do you have the most control?

Self-Communication

Do you ask yourself, What is my lesson here? What am I supposed to learn? How and why have I attracted this situation into my life? What gift is being offered? What do I need to learn to be able to handle this situation effectively?

Appreciation

Do you appreciate your child's "misbehavior," knowing there is a lesson in it for you as well as for him or her? What is your attitude toward the choices your children make and the behavior they exhibit? Are you resentful, angry, controlling, threatened? When you are looking for an answer to a problem, do you invite suggestions from your children, regardless of their age? Are you willing to accept direction from your children? Do you see value in their telling you what to do or say?

Belief

Do you believe that children have a contribution to make right now, at their current age? Do you believe that children should be seen and not heard, should listen and not comment, should answer and not question, should do and not direct? Do you believe that children intuitively know what they need to learn, or must they be told/taught everything?

Managing Your Mind

How do you go about remembering that your child is the teacher

and that you are the student? Do you remind yourself frequently that a lesson for you exists within each conflict? Do you move up before you move in? Do you ask, What is it that I need to know?, and open yourself to learning it?

Value

Do you see your children as a gift to you and to the world? Do you value their opinions? Do you encourage the expression of feelings and allow your children opportunities to vent? Do you see them as a blessing, regardless of their behavior, disposition, or disability? Do you welcome the lessons your children offer you through the behavior they exhibit?

Conclusion

The traditional vision of parenting focuses on filling children's minds with information, managing their behavior, and expecting them to master a set of predetermined skills. The ninth commitment's perspective is quite different. You are asked to consider yourself as the student and your child as the teacher. Your children have become a part of your life, in part, so you can learn from them. Your role is not always to guide but, at times, to be led.

The ninth commitment also calls on you to see your children as their own teacher. Children know what they need to learn. They become involved in the world in a variety of ways to facilitate their own learning. They explore and discover what it is they need to become fully who and what they are meant to be. They often guide their own process.

Seeing your children as teacher empowers them to stretch and learn in ways you do not see. It promotes growth and maturation, both for them and for you.

The Tenth Commitment

I commit to creating a sense of oneness in my family.

I am present for my children, helping them develop roots and feelings of belonging. I treat my children with love and caring. I create a sense of oneness in my family.

A hundred years ago, parents didn't have to work at building family solidarity. Togetherness and oneness just happened. It occurred because of forced interdependence. Family members were forced to care about each other for their individual and collective survival. Everyone was needed to sustain the family economically. Sons worked in the fields with their fathers. Daughters worked side by side with their mothers. Children received continuous on the job training for adulthood.

Young people no longer have a significant role to play in many families. Sadly, today's child is seldom an observer, much less a participant, in important family matters.

What we used to refer to as the traditional family, one parent working while the other stays home, is no longer the norm. Over half of all marriages now end in divorce. Over 25 percent of children live with one parent. Most often, that parent is the mother. One-fourth of all children have no one to meet them when they get home from school. Eight thousand new stepfamilies form each week. The fastest growing family unit is grandparents raising their grandchildren. Extended family members used to live in close proximity. Now they are often scattered all across the country.

Because of the changing nature of the family and the weakening of essential support systems, many parents wonder if it's possible to help their children develop any meaningful roots. The essential question becomes, *Can family solidarity and creating a sense of oneness be created and maintained today?*

Creating a feeling of belonging and oneness in your family is possible, and it doesn't just happen—not by luck, coincidence, or happenstance. Togetherness occurs in families when the adults in that family work with intentionality to create it. It requires parents who value family unity and place it high on their list of priorities. It takes effort, energy, time, and skills. It demands an allegiance to the tenth commitment.

At the center of the tenth commitment is the goal of developing a sense of connectedness through placing the family first. While independence is important in childhood development, so too is belonging. When one feels connected to a larger unit (a family), a sense of security is created. Individuals are then safe to explore and challenge themselves independently within the security of the family structure.

Family is a place where teasing about one's hairstyle or recent social blunder is not permitted. Jokes about one's fears or shortcomings are not tolerated. Members of the family are embraced and celebrated for their differences. It is within the security of a loving family that one can feel safe to try new things, make mistakes, and discover the self.

The tenth commitment is operating in your family when family members feel closeness and affection for each other. This commitment has to do with feeling that you are a part of something larger than yourself and identifying with that group. The family is a place where members experience connectedness, can count on each other, and believe, *We're all in this together*.

When the members of a family believe they are all standing together, the goal of placing *family first* can be realized. Decisions

are then made with the needs and wants of all in mind. Everyone has input, from the youngest to the oldest. A decision is reached in the family's best interest. One person does not get what they want every time, and the notion that a majority rules is not always employed.

By placing your family first, you teach your children that people are more important than things. As each family member has the opportunity to feel connected through the support, encouragement, and understanding of others in the family, he or she begins to realize that people are valued over objects and rigid rules. Making sure the grass is mowed or the house is cleaned or the garbage is out is not as important as playing soccer in the backyard with your daughter, listening to your teenage son tell you about his date last night, or rocking your baby to sleep.

When your daughter hits her younger brother out of frustration and you rush to the aid of your son first, you send an important message. When you console him before correcting your daughter's behavior, you are teaching both of your children that people's feelings have value. You are demonstrating the principle that people are more important than implementing discipline strategies. When you go to your son first, your daughter is not being reinforced for her aggressive behavior but being shown where value is placed in your family—on the feelings and well-being of individual family members.

A child's motivation to behave does not come from fear of punishment. It comes from being in a relationship. Being connected to a family and feeling that connection in one's heart and soul is what helps a child manage his or her own behavior. Children desire to be a part of the family when people are more important than things and the emphasis is on family first.

One effective way to build feelings of belonging and develop a sense of oneness in your family is through the use of rituals. Rituals contain the myths, history, identity, and purpose of the family. When rituals are practiced with frequency and intensity, they create connectedness.

A ritual can be almost any activity that the family engages in regularly. It can be big or small. It can be expensive or cost nothing. It can be connected to a holiday or not. What makes an activity a ritual is the repetition and the drama that elevates it above ordinary activities. Eating a meal is an everyday activity that can be elevated to ritual status when the family gathers every Sunday morning to eat personalized omelets, made to order, by Dad. Taking the time to read a book with your child wouldn't be a ritual in and of itself. Reading a chapter in a special book together on Saturday morning becomes a ritual when it occurs regularly over time.

A ritual does not require props, crowds, or special training to perform. Singing a song as you clean up the toys in the playroom could be a ritual. Making popcorn every Friday night as the family sits down to watch a video is a ritual. Saying a special prayer together with your child every night as you tuck her into bed is a ritual. Having a special dinner every time someone has a birthday is a ritual.

Creating a sense of oneness by using rituals involves identifying an activity the family finds enjoyable and repeating it over and over. Search your family life for everyday happenings that are fun, relaxing, creative, exciting, or educational. Can that activity be repeated frequently? If so, it may make a great ritual. Create rituals that are unique to your family. Your children will remember them for the rest of their lives.

Another way of putting the tenth commitment to work in your family life is to preserve its history. Children require a deep feeling of connection to their past or heritage in order to sink roots. When these human roots grow deep, they hold the child firm, creating stability.

Begin by keeping a recorded history of your family. Take photos and arrange them chronologically. A shoebox or desk drawer does not work for this purpose. It requires more organization. Large photo albums work well. Along with photos of vacation trips,

birthdays, athletic events, and other significant happenings, mix in samples of schoolwork, postcards from grandparents, or printed memorabilia from events you have attended.

When several albums have accumulated, display them in a place of importance in your home. Enhance this "nostalgia corner" by adding baby books, memorabilia, journals, etc. This is also an ideal place to store family folklore, including the myths, folktales, or special stories pertinent to your family. Invite your own parents to record some of the folklore they remember on tape or in writing so their stories are preserved.

Create a file of schoolwork for each child to add to your nostalgia corner. By preserving special papers in a systematic way, children can return to them repeatedly over time to see their growth. When they look at their work on math problems, creative writing, or penmanship on a daily basis, it's difficult for them to notice growth and improvement. Watching the products of their work over time allows them to observe their progress and accomplishment.

In recommending the preservation of family history, it is not our intention to encourage children to live in the past but to provide a way for them to recall the past, recognize how it evolves into the present, and project a positive future. "I *had* an important place in this family. I *have* an important place in this family. I expect I *will have* an important place in this family." These are important connections we want our children to make to strengthen their feeling of belonging.

Life Examples

Jason Williams uses symbolism to support connectedness in his family. On special occasions that involve food, he splits an apple, orange, or candy bar into as many pieces as there are family members. The family then eats the food, using this symbolic gesture to help members realize it takes all the individual parts to make one whole.

*****

Brenda and Charlie Cotts pulled up roots when their children, Sarah and Michelle, were six and eight years old. They moved from Portland, Oregon, to Petoskey, Michigan. Both children changed schools. Both parents changed jobs. All four of them changed houses.

On the day of the move, after the moving van had been packed and was on its way, Brenda and Charlie took their two girls back into the house to say a final goodbye. Leaving the house represented a loss, a big loss, to all of them, and these parents knew that it was important to get closure on this piece of their lives before they moved on.

Brenda and Charlie spread a blanket on the living room floor and had the family sit in a circle facing each other. "Let's go around the circle and each share one of our favorite memories about living here," Charlie suggested. The four of them then took turns telling stories about the day the dog chewed Charlie's shoes, the nights the family spent in the backyard looking at stars and searching for satellites, the time Sarah came home from the hospital, the addition of the back porch.

"Now let's tell something we're going to miss about this home," Brenda suggested. Each of the Cotts shared something special about living in the house they were leaving: the swing in the backyard, the remodeled kitchen, the fireside chats, the big closets.

Tears were shed during this ceremony. There was sadness as well as laughter. When the sharing ended, the family stood in the middle of the living room and enjoyed a family hug accompanied by more tears.

One by one, as they were ready, the Cotts climbed into their packed SUV. As they drove away, they all waved a final goodbye to the house they had known and loved for several years.

*****

Carla Perez's right leg swung forward with equal amounts of force and precision. Her foot connected squarely with the soccer ball and sent it on an arching path over the goalie's head, under the crossbar, and into the net. The goal, her first in 43 American Youth Soccer Organization games, was greeted with the traditional backslaps, high fives, and wide grins.

The spontaneous 90-second celebration that followed Carla's goal was warm and genuine. It acknowledged her individual accomplishment as well as the total team effort. But, more important for the Perez family, the goal was a signal that it was time to observe one of their favorite family rituals, for Carla had just achieved a First.

Firsts. The term has special meaning in the Perez family and is cause for celebration. "Firsts" are any event, success, or goal achievement that occurs for the first time. Firsts are benchmarks in family members' lives that signal an active participation in life and a willingness to take risks. They are visible reminders of growth. As such, Carla's parents feel they deserve special recognition.

Some Firsts the Perezes have recognized include: their older son, Timo, pitching a shutout; Roberto learning how to read; Carla getting on the honor roll; Mr. Perez getting a promotion; and Roberto learning to ride his bike.

Each First is celebrated in a specific way, for a specific reason. The Perez family showcases Firsts by going out to dinner together. The individual who achieves the First becomes the focus person. He or she chooses both the time and place for the celebration. At the appointed time, the entire family gathers to share a meal, acknowledge the individual, and practice collective caring. The focus person takes the spotlight and tells about his or her special moment, communicating feelings, reactions, impressions, or any new goals he or she has set. The rest of the family listens without interrupting the narrative.

When the focus person has finished sharing, other family

members participate by telling what they liked about either the First or the reaction of the person who achieved it. Informal conversation follows until the conclusion of their celebration.

Celebrating Firsts helps the Perez family achieve two important goals simultaneously. It allows them to connect as a family as well as celebrate the uniqueness of the person being honored. They hope you will steal this idea and use it with your family. But remember: they did it first.

*****

Shannon's stepfather, Jerry Dyer, travels frequently as part of his profession. While away, he stays connected to his stepdaughter by using one of her passions—horses.

Whenever he is off on a business trip, Jerry finds a postcard of a horse and mails it to his stepdaughter along with a warm greeting. Sometimes he gets home before the postcard arrives. At other times, the postcard beats him.

Over the past five years, Shannon has filled a shoebox with horse postcards. They show pictures of Arabians, quarter horses, Appaloosas, and Morgans, as well as other breeds. The cards also include pictures of Native Americans, jockeys, farmers, soldiers, fox hunters, and cowboys. Some horses are full grown. Others are foals. Some are wild. Others are domesticated.

At last count, Shannon had accumulated 317 postcards of horses, each with a message from her stepfather. On occasion, Shannon and Jerry take the postcards out and organize them on the kitchen table. They make a pile of their top ten favorites and take turns telling why they selected each one. They talk about the funny ones and what it might be like to live in that period of time or part of the country.

Home or away, the horse postcards help Shannon and her stepdad connect.

*****

Some parents see New Year's Eve as an opportunity to get away from the family to celebrate in private or with friends. Going out to dinner, attending parties, and emptying bottles seems to be the order of the night. Another alternative, one that can help your family grow closer, is to spend New Year's Eve together. That's what the Lowrys do. They see New Year's Eve as an ideal time to celebrate connectedness, reflect on the past year, and look ahead to the future.

For the Lowrys, deciding what treats to purchase, shopping together, and decorating as a family occupy much of the day. Dinner and card games fill the early evening. When interest in games dies down, they assemble in the living room, sit in a circle, and begin the most meaningful part of their New Year's Eve together: Topic Talk.

Topics are ideas they dream up to structure the family conversation. One family member suggests a topic like "A new friend I made this year" or "My favorite song this year." The Lowrys then each take a turn responding to the topic for as long as they wish. Listeners do simply that—listen. When each person has had an opportunity to respond to the topic, family members ask questions and elaborate on their remarks. Topics used in the past that have helped the Lowrys get in touch with each other and reflect on the previous year include: "My favorite book this year," "Something I did that I'm proud of," "Something I wish I could do over," "My favorite place I visited this year," "Something I bought for myself," "Something I did for others."

At 11 o'clock, the Lowrys end Topic Talk and get out Our Goals, the list of goals the family recorded a year earlier. Each member takes a turn reading his or her goals from the preceding year and telling whether the goals were accomplished. One New Year's Eve the goals were:

Jerry: Go to horseback riding camp.

Matt: Get a medal in wrestling.

Brenda: Make the high school softball team.

Mr. Lowry: Run a marathon with dignity.

Mrs. Lowry: Lose 30 pounds.

After sharing how they did on the previous year's goals, the Lowrys create new goals for the coming year. Jerry acts as recorder and takes down each family member's contribution. The new goals are put away until the next New Year's Eve celebration.

As the time nears midnight, the Lowrys turn on the TV and count down the minutes and seconds until the New Year arrives. The traditional hugs, kisses, and noisemaking follow.

*****

When Mr. Ashcroft's two sons were in fifth and sixth grades, both of their teachers commented on the sad state of the boys' penmanship. Being a former teacher himself, Mr. Ashcroft believed that one of the best ways to improve penmanship is to practice, but he didn't want his children to sit and do formal penmanship sessions, forming the same letters over and over. So he offered his sons a deal. He agreed to extend each child's bedtime by one-half hour if he would agree to write in a journal for ten minutes of that time. Both boys agreed. Spiral notebooks were purchased for the project.

Each night, when the boys finished writing, they would bring their journals to their father before they went to bed. He would write a few sentences in response and leave the journals by their bedroom door for them to find in the morning. This journal activity was not used to correct spelling or punctuation or to comment on penmanship. It was used to build relationships. It was a way to connect.

Mr. Ashcroft found that his children would often put in writing what they would not say aloud. Responding in journals gave him an

opportunity to think through what he wanted to say and to share parts of himself with his children.

Over time, the boys' penmanship improved. So did the relationship between a father and his sons.

*****

Frank Thomas took his two daughters to school every morning, and he was not enjoying it. Neither, it seemed, were the girls. The 20-minute ride would begin with an argument about who would sit where. It continued with further arguments about what song to listen to on the radio or who saw the yellow truck first or what was the best topping on a pizza.

One day, in the midst of his daughters' arguing over what type of animal was smaller, a vole or a shrew, Frank interjected, "I know a story about a vole and a mouse and a big barn cat." The excitement in Frank's voice caught the girls' attention.

Frank began to create a scene off the top of his head, telling the story as he drove. Not knowing their father was making the story up as it unfolded in his mind, the girls grew quiet and listened. Encouraged by their interest, Frank kept adding to the tale until they reached the school. To peak the girls' interest, he ended the story in mid-sentence with the mouse trapped in a corner by the barn cat. "I guess we'll have to hear the rest tomorrow," he teased.

To Frank's surprise, the next morning the girls were sitting quietly in the back seat when he got into the car. He barely made it to the end of the driveway before the oldest broke the silence. "Well," she said, "tell us the rest of the story. What happens to the mouse?" Frank smiled and picked up the story where he had left off the day before.

From that day on, every morning on the way to school Frank told another part of the mouse story. The girls became so involved they began offering ideas for new storylines and making suggestions

for new characters. By the end of the school year, Frank and the girls had created over 25 new animal characters and many additional adventures of Fred, the mouse.

Today, 20 years later, Frank and his adult daughters are writing the stories they created on the way to school and plan to publish a series of chapter books for first- and second-grade readers.

*****

Arthur had an appointment with a local attorney to discuss a legal matter regarding his property up north. Not totally trusting lawyers, he didn't look forward to their first meeting.

When he entered Mr. Tillman's office, Arthur noted the professional credentials and diplomas on the wall. He was impressed by the massive display of the lawyer's accomplishments and felt intimidated until a mahogany plaque in the middle of all the other neatly framed items caught his eye. It was inscribed with the words: SUCCEED AT HOME FIRST.

Arthur began to relax. He liked the fact that the plaques informing clients of Mr. Tillman's professional accomplishments were placed around the one that told of the importance of his family. Arthur knew then that their professional relationship would be long and mutually satisfactory.

*****

Following the remodeling of their home, Clark and Susan Ricket decided that extra care would be needed to maintain the new wood floor. They called a family meeting to discuss the matter and develop a plan that would be easy for the entire family to implement.

During the meeting, all three children and their parents agreed that the new wood floor was beautiful and that changes would need to be made to preserve its luster. The frequency of sweeping

and washing it was discussed, as well as the use of toys on the floor. It was agreed upon by all that shoes would no longer be worn in the house, and a spot was created by the back door for everyone's shoes.

A few days later, four-year-old Hunter, the youngest member of the Ricket family, asked to have another family meeting about the wood floor. That evening all five members gathered to hear Hunter's concerns.

"I keep slipping on this floor," Hunter told them.

"Take your socks off," his older brother, Andrew, suggested.

"But my feet will get cold."

"You could wear your slippers, as long as you didn't wear them outside, too," his mother told him.

"Hey, can we all get nice indoor slippers to wear?" asked Darlene, the middle child.

"I don't see why not," Mr. Ricket responded. "We'll all go slipper shopping this weekend."

The following Saturday afternoon, as planned, the family ventured out together in search of the perfect slippers for each person's feet. After they had all made their selections, everyone went home excited about trying out their footwear purchases on the new floor. The slippers were a huge success. Slipping on the floor was no longer a concern.

Two weeks passed and Hunter asked again to hold a family meeting about the wood floor. Once again, the family gathered. This time Hunter was concerned about guests at the house. With a worried look, he said, "When other people come to our house they won't have slippers to wear. They might slip and fall."

"What can we do about that?" Mrs. Ricket asked.

"We can buy a bunch of slippers and keep them in a box by the door," Darlene suggested.

"That would be a lot of slippers to buy to get a size for everyone," their father noted.

"Maybe we shouldn't enforce the 'no shoes' rule for guests who are concerned about slipping on the wood floor," Andrew said.

Everyone agreed with Andrew's idea, knowing that the family placed great value on safety and on having people feel comfortable while in their home.

Hunter, for the time being, was satisfied with the wood floor situation. But everyone knew that if his satisfaction changed he would be calling another family meeting in the future.

The Oneness Commitment

Are you committed to creating a feeling of belonging and togetherness in your family? Check over the areas below. Determine if you are where you want to be as a parent in respect to each category. Use the information to celebrate your successes or set new goals for yourself.

Creation

Are you creating the "our family" feeling or the "my family" feeling with your parenting techniques? Do you more often use the words I/me/my or us/we/our? Do you attempt to create a shared control style of family management, or do you run the show with little input from other family members? Do you include strategies to build family unity on your "to do" list, or do you leave that important issue to chance?

Modeling

Do you model closeness and affection for your children? Do you hug frequently or only on special occasions? Do you connect with your children through sustained eye contact? Do you smile

frequently? Do you schedule private time with each of your children to go for walks, bike rides, or a swing in the park? How many minutes per day do you engage in conversation where you invest as much time in listening as you do in speaking?

Play

Do you play regularly with your children? Do you see play as a frivolous waste of time or as an investment in connecting with them? Do you insist they play the way you want to play, or can you let them take the lead and play in their style? Do you insist that play be an opportunity for learning academic skills, or can you allow playtime to be playtime and trust that the academics will take care of themselves?

Preservation

Are you actively working to preserve the traditions of your family? Have you created a family tree? Do you have a nostalgia corner in your home? Are there favorite family stories that get retold frequently? Do you look for opportunities to add to the folklore that is part of your family history?

Rituals

Do you invest time in creating and observing rituals that your family can look forward to with anticipation? Will you create memories to pass on to future generations by establishing a ritual that recognizes special events or shared family values? Do you use rituals to cultivate a knowledge and appreciation of cultural heritage?

Priority

Do you see your family as a priority, or do you strive to succeed at work first? Is *doing for* the family more important than *being with* the family? Do you place family first? Does your behavior match your beliefs?

Conclusion

You can strengthen family unity and help your children sink roots whether you are a single parent, live with a spouse of 15 years, or see your children only on weekends. You can produce a sense of oneness by creating a plan and systematically following it with discipline and a strong belief in its importance.

Use the ideas in this and other chapters as a guide. It is not our intention to suggest they are *the* way. Every family is unique. Each family must develop its own way. The concepts presented here can serve as a beacon light to point the direction. Use them to guide you. Adopt them, adapt them, delete and add to them. Enjoy the process of strengthening family unity *your* way.

ABOUT THE AUTHORS

Portraits by Gregg

Chick Moorman

Chick Moorman is the director of the Institute for Personal Power, a consulting firm dedicated to providing high-quality professional development activities for educators and parents.

He is a former classroom teacher with over 40 years of experience in the field of education. His mission is to help people experience a greater sense of personal power in their lives so they can in turn empower others.

Chick conducts full-day workshops and seminars for school districts and parent groups. He also delivers keynote addresses for local, state, and national conferences.

He is available for the following topic areas:

FOR EDUCATORS

- Achievement Motivation and Behavior Management through Effective Teacher Talk
- Teaching Respect and Responsibility
- Improving Student Self-Esteem
- Stamping Out Learned Helplessness
- Cooperative Learning
- Celebrate the Spirit Whisperers
- Dealing with Reluctant Learners

FOR PARENTS

- The 10 Commitments
- Parent Talk: Words That Empower, Words That Wound
- Raising Your Child's Self-Esteem
- Empowered Parenting
- Building Family Solidarity
- Raising Response-Able Children

If you would like more information about these programs or would like to discuss a possible training or speaking date, please contact:

Chick Moorman
P.O. Box 547
Merrill, MI 48637
Telephone: (877) 360-1477
Fax: (989) 643-5156
E-mail: ipp57@aol.com
Website: www.chickmoorman.com

Portraits by Gregg

Thomas B. Haller, MDiv, MSW, ACSW, DST

Thomas Haller currently works in private practice at Shinedling, Shinedling, and Haller, P.C., in Bay City, Michigan, as a child, adolescent, and couples therapist; an individual psychotherapist; and a chronic pain counselor. He is a certified EEG biofeedback technician, an AASECT Certified Diplomate of Sex Therapy, and a certified sports counselor. Thomas has extensive training in psychotherapy with children and couples from the University of Michigan, where he received his Master of Social Work degree. He is also an ordained Lutheran minister with a Master of Divinity degree from Concordia Theological Seminary.

Thomas is a widely sought-after national and international presenter in the areas of parenting, interpersonal relationships, and chronic

pain. He is also the founder and director of Healing Minds Institute, a center devoted to teaching others how to enhance the health of their mind, body, and spirit.

Thomas conducts workshops and seminars for churches, school districts, parent groups, and counseling agencies. He is also a regular lecturer atuniversities across the country.

He is available for the following topic areas:

FOR COUPLES

- The Balance of Autonomy and Boundaries
- How to Talk to Your Partner about Sex
- How to Talk to Your Partner in Language That Builds Mutual Respect and Intimacy
- The Language of Feelings in Committed Relationships
- Response-Able Partnering

FOR PARENTS

- The 10 Commitments
- Managing Aggression and Anger in Children
- The Parent Talk Experience
- How to Talk to Your Children about Sex
- Creating a Caring Environment in the Home
- Understanding Your Children's Feelings

FOR EDUCATORS

- Brain Functioning and Behavior in Children
- Transforming Aggression in Children
- Creating a Caring Environment in the Classroom
- Understanding Asperger's Syndrome

For more information about these programs or to discuss a possible training or speaking date, please contact:

Thomas Haller
Shinedling, Shinedling, and Haller, P.C.
2355 ½ Delta Rd.
Bay City, MI 48706
Telephone: (989) 667-5654
Fax: (989) 667-5330
E-mail: thomas@thomashaller.com
Website: www.thomashaller.com

Photo by David Dellar

OUR VISION: HEALING ACRES

A portion of the proceeds from *The 10 Commitments: Parenting with Purpose* will be used to create an equine retirement ranch. One dollar from each book sold will go toward the creation and support of **Healing Acres Equine Retirement Ranch.**

The goal of Healing Acres Ranch is to provide a peaceful and caring environment for aged horses that have devoted many years of service. It will include a low-stress atmosphere, room to exercise and graze freely, adequate shelter, and preventive and attentive health care for all horses.

Other services planned for Healing Acres Ranch include therapeutic riding for persons with disabilities and equine-assisted psychotherapy.

If you wish to make a donation beyond the purchase of this book, please visit our website: www.healingacres.com

Thank you for helping us support this vision.

OTHER BOOKS AND PRODUCTS

COUPLE TALK: How to Talk Your Way to a Great Relationship, by Chick Moorman and Thomas Haller ($25.00)

SPIRIT WIIISPERERS: Teachers Who Nourish a Child's Spirit, by Chick Moorman ($25.00)

PARENT TALK: How to Talk to Your Children in Language That Builds Self-Esteem and Encourages Responsibility, by Chick Moorman ($13.00)

TEACHER TALK: What It Really Means, by Chick Moorman and Nancy Weber ($13.00)

WHERE THE HEART IS: Stories of Home and Family, by Chick Moorman ($15.00)

TALK SENSE TO YOURSELF: The Language of Personal Power, by Chick Moorman ($13.00)

OUR CLASSROOM: We Can Learn Together, by Chick Moorman and Dee Dishon ($20.00)

THE LANGUAGE OF RESPONSE-ABLE PARENTING, audiocassette series featuring Chick Moorman ($39.50)